TEACHER
Coaching

DEDICATION

To my wonderful parents, Vanessa and Tony, for showing me the importance of good relationships.

TEACHER Coaching

Kirsty Stokes

First published in 2024 by Critical Publishing Ltd

Published 2025 by Routledge
4 Park Square, Milton Park, Abingdon, Oxon OX14 4RN
605 Third Avenue, New York, NY 10017

Routledge is an imprint of the Taylor & Francis Group, an informa business

Copyright © 2024 Kirsty Stokes

All rights reserved. No part of this book may be reprinted or reproduced or utilised in any form or by any electronic, mechanical, or other means, now known or hereafter invented, including photocopying and recording, or in any information storage or retrieval system, without permission in writing from the publishers.

Trademark notice: Product or corporate names may be trademarks or registered trademarks, and are used only for identification and explanation without intent to infringe.

British Library Cataloguing in Publication Data
A CIP record for this book is available from the British Library

ISBN: 9781041057246 (hbk)
ISBN: 9781915713780 (pbk)
ISBN: 9781041057253 (ebk)

The right of Kirsty Stokes to be identified as the Author of this work has been asserted by her in accordance with the Copyright, Design and Patents Act 1988.

Text design by Greensplash
Cover design by Out of House Limited

DOI: 10.4324/9781041057253

Give a man a fish and you feed him for day. Teach a man to fish and you feed him for a lifetime.
                                                                    Chinese proverb

If you wish to get the most out of this book, there is one indispensable requirement, one essentially infinitely important rule more than any technique. Unless you have this one fundamental requisite, a thousand rules on how to study will avail little. And if you do have this cardinal endowment, then you can achieve wonders without reading any suggestions for getting the most out of a book. What is this magic requirement? Just this: a deep, driving desire to learn, a vigorous determination to increase your ability to deal with people.
                        Dale Carnegie, 2019, Foreword quote from
                            How to Win Friends and Influence People
                                                        (Carnegie, 2023)

About this book

The purpose of this book is to introduce the TEACHER coaching model in the hope that more teachers and pupils will benefit from the power of coaching.

A percentage of profits from the sale of this book supports the Tim Henman Foundation.

The Tim Henman Foundation is a youth charity with the mission of transforming the lives of disadvantaged young people by creating sporting and educational opportunities as well as improving mental and physical health together with our partners.

It delivers sports programmes, which break down access and financial barriers to allow young people the opportunity to participate and progress.

Its education programmes provide opportunities for students who require extra support and young people who wish to progress their career paths.

CONTENTS

About the author		ix
A brief introduction		xi
Chapter 1:	Coaching: What is it?	1
Chapter 2:	A brief history of coaching	21
Chapter 3:	The case for coaching	39
Chapter 4:	The TEACHER coaching model	59
Chapter 5:	Implementing a coaching culture	105
Chapter 6:	Being a coach	125
A final note on TEACHER coaching		147
References		155
Index		169

About the author

Kirsty Stokes is a teacher, coach and sports coach who has been involved in education since 1995, when coaching was in its infancy. She has taught for over 20 years, in nine schools across the entire age range and in both the public and private sectors, incorporating coaching techniques and leading the development of coaching in staff appraisals. She is currently Director of Studies at a preparatory school.

A brief introduction

Are you a happy and fulfilled teacher?

Is everyone around you also happy and fulfilled, and living life to their full potential?

If yes ...

Skip to the part that says 'Phew! You've made it to the end.'

If no ...

Read on to see how you can find out more about coaching, how it can be used in schools and how you can use coaching to develop yourself and other teachers.

Read on to learn about the TEACHER coaching model and how it can be used for happier and more effective appraisals, as well as how you can introduce others to TEACHER coaching through critical thinking discussions.

Chapter 1:
COACHING: WHAT IS IT?

> **LEARNING OBJECTIVES**
>
> - To help you understand what coaching is.
> - To explain how it is different from mentoring.
> - To identify different definitions of coaching.
> - To demonstrate that there are spectrums of teaching and coaching styles.
> - To introduce you to the TEACHER coaching model.

What is coaching?

Martin Underwood was a kind and lovely man. He was also an amazing lecturer at Exeter University. In one lecture he set the challenge of creating a mnemonic for remembering different teaching styles. I know I didn't win, but he liked my effort of **CRISP** **L**ike **G**olden **D**elicious.

This mnemonic reflected the ideas written in the book *The Spectrum of Teaching Styles for Physical Education* as proposed and written by Muska Mosston. Despite the great efforts of his former student, and later colleague, Sara Ashworth in continuing and developing it, Mosston's work has not achieved the same recognition in university teacher education courses as that of John Dewey, Jean Piaget or Howard Gardner. Yet I think it should.

Thirty years later, I still remember what my mnemonic stood for:

- **C**ommand;
- **R**eciprocal;
- **I**nclusion;
- **S**elf-check;
- **Pr**actice style;
- **L**earner designed and initiated;
- **G**uided discovery;
- **D**ivergent style.

Convergent and divergent are both discovery styles using open-ended questions. Mosston tweaked his spectrum over the years, but I think the convergent teaching style was also in the original lineup, despite me not including it – possibly the reason why my mnemonic did not win! The spectrum starts with the teacher-centred command style and ends with the student-centred, learner-designed and initiated teaching styles. The spectrum has been amended further to include self-teaching. In command style, the teacher directs all the learning and makes all the decisions with little or no input from the learner. An example might be drill instruction in public schools for the nineteenth-century concept of muscular Christianity. I was going to suggest the PE teacher in the 1969 film *Kes* as a further example, but it might be difficult to focus on his use of command style among all his pedagogical errors! Watch a clip if you don't know what I mean, or just imagine balls being thrown at children. A better example might be issuing safety instructions for adventurous activities. At the other end of the spectrum, learners are given open-ended problems or tasks and encouraged to explore.

Many other scholars have been linked with the use of the word 'coaching' as it is used today, in both schools and industry, but I like to think Mosston had a hand in shaping our understanding. Mosston spent his life working out ways to get the best out of people, and his later approaches focused on autonomy, an individual's motivations, goal-setting and reflective practice. Mosston's student-centred approaches thus appear to be coaching styles.

The power of coaching

Coaching is about relationships. Whether it is within a business or school setting, and whether the relationships are between staff and pupils, or between staff members, or even between pupils, coaching helps to create and nurture good working relationships through its focus on people and good conversations.

Coaching involves autonomy. It focuses on input from the coachee (the person being coached) and requires that they be helped to design their own plan for improvement. Autonomy can increase motivation, but the coach can also help the coachee with further motivational techniques.

Coaching in organisations, including schools, helps build a culture where it is okay to fail as you can learn from your mistakes, that relationships, trust and empathy are important, that growth is important, and that community is important as people close to you care about you and want you to develop. Coaching is also about the power of having goals, creating and following plans and the importance of taking time to reflect.

Implementing coaching across a school or organisation helps to create a coaching culture, and the culture helps to support further coaching. A culture embedded with coaching helps individuals, teams and organisations develop and reach their potential. You cannot just pay lip service to coaching. You need to believe in its power. A commitment is required from everyone, at all levels in the organisation. I've worked in a school where people have spoken about the 'magic' of the school, and how you should try and 'bottle up' what it develops – this describes a great culture.

A coaching culture requires fostering collaboration, trust and respect, and it involves individuals wanting to take responsibility for their own learning. A coaching culture means you have a more positive climate and a happier community where individuals experience greater subjective well-being, leading to a more motivated and productive workforce and more successful learners.

Definitions of coaching

The word 'coach' comes from the word *Kocs* (pronounced 'kotch'), a Hungarian village where horse-drawn coaches were introduced in the fifteenth century. By the nineteenth century, similar coaches were used in Great Britain for carrying goods and passengers, but the term was also coined by Oxford University to describe how tutors would coach, or give individualised instruction or guidance, to 'carry' a student through an exam.

Since these early uses of the word 'coach', there has been an intertwined history of the development of the pedagogy of teaching, the history of coaching and mentoring, and the history and development of the fields of counselling, psychology and philosophy. Much debate could go into how each field shaped the next, how each field has developed and how certain lines between the fields have blurred, but this is another discussion. Coaching principles and practices, for whatever reasons, have developed over the years. 'Coaching' has been a term used in the education system for many years, but mainly through its use on the sports field. However, coaching principles are also now practised in other areas in forward-thinking educational settings.

There are numerous definitions of coaching, and its definition has morphed alongside the creation of different coaching models. Coaching is a tool designed to get the best out of organisations and individuals, and enhance performance. Gallwey explains that coaching is about unlocking a person's potential to maximise their own performance. Coaching is practised in many industries, and the education system seems to be somewhat behind in its adoption of coaching practices. Luckily, we are starting to catch up.

Coaching is a process where the coach guides the coachee to fulfil their potential and unlock their natural ability, and where the coachee has ownership of their own development. It is a motivating discussion in which the coach has a positive influence and the coachee has their personal ability enhanced through guided self-discovery. Coaching involves motivation, and the coach helps the coachee to remain motivated on their journey of self-discovery and motivated to commit to their goal. Coaching is encouraging, but it is far more than just a sports coach rubbing the shoulders of a player and motivating them for the second half.

Coaching involves the setting of a goal or goals and the formation of a plan. It is often task focused. It can be used for specific skills or performance development and can involve a short-term relationship between the coach and coachee. The coach learns the values of the coachee, and then their job is *'to forward and deepen'* and although the coachee is selecting their goal, it is the coach's role to select *'the tools and manage the time and structure of the coaching session'* (Kimsey-House et al, 2011, p 81). The coach and the coachee develop a partnership to help the coachee progress.

Coaching also involves feedback and the requirement for a growth mindset. If you are to set yourself a goal, you need to know your strengths and weaknesses. Whitmore writes that *'feedback from ourselves and others is vital for learning and performance improvement'* and *'coaching delivers ... because of the supportive relationship between the coach and coachee, and the means and style of communication used'* (Whitmore, 2002, p 7).

Despite their kinaesthetic awareness, and the fact that dancers use mirrors in studios to help with feedback, they still can't see if their own leg is in a perfect arabesque behind them while still keeping their line; feedback from others is important too. The same applies outside of sporting contexts: feedback helps people improve.

Coaching is about empowerment and autonomy. Coaching is *'a way of effectively empowering people to find their own answers, encouraging them and supporting them on the path'* (Kimsey-House et al, 2011, p 16). The coachee is guided to develop a flexible plan to achieve their desired goal. The objective of the coach is to support and guide the coachee to find their own solutions and actions towards their chosen goal. Girling (2021) explains that coaching is about helping people to explore their own ideas. Coaching allows more ownership and freedom of choice to the individual. This is important as Brehm's 1960s' theory on psychological reactance (Brehm and Brehm, 2013) tells us that people can have negative reactions when they think their freedom is limited. Dorrance Hall (2019) also discusses direct restoration, which she explains is when we choose to rebel, in response to being told what to do. According to MacLennan (2017), directing people to do something has always achieved inferior results compared with inspiring them to act, and skilful coaching can inspire those in an organisation. If you need motivation, watch the Chris Hemsworth YouTube clip *You Got This*; if you need inspiration to act, this will certainly help!

Coaching also involves reflection, and reviewing and improving plans and actions. Coaching is a process of development where the coachee is guided and supported through a conversation in order to improve, as opposed to being told what to do. The coachee may gain clarity and perspective though their discussions, but they need to reflect on their own performance throughout the coaching cycle, from goal-setting to actioning goals and reflecting on progress. The coach needs to be aware of their supportive and guiding role, but they also need to reflect on the situation and to consider progress and what coaching skills to implement.

Coaching is cyclical. A coaching cycle describes a plan for the communication between the coach and coachee, allowing for input from both, in order to improve performance. The cycle involves various stages including building a trusting relationship, discussing feedback, discussing goals, planning actions and reviewing progress.

On sports fields, coaching practices can be developed where pupils are set open tasks, create their own individual goals and action plans, and encouraged to commit to their plan and reflect on their progress. However, coaching can have numerous other uses in an educational setting. In a form, or academic tutor role, coaching can be used as a holistic approach to pupils' growth and development. Coaching, despite sometimes being called tutoring, is seen in Pre-Senior Baccalaureate (PSB) schools and is a key part of their education. The PSB is an assessment model that has at its heart the development of the right values, skills, attitudes and behaviours required for children to flourish in an ever-changing world. Coaching helps pupils achieve this, whether they are young people or adults. Coaching addresses the whole person, their emotional well-being, their beliefs, values and aspirations, as the coachee sets their own, individual goals and plans – which might be set for a multitude of reasons. Coaching can help a coachee with their learning and development, to improve skill or performance or to help a coachee explore their own beliefs, attitudes and values. Coaching can be a link between pastoral and academic development, or between personal and work life. It can be an approach for longer term goal-setting for a pupil or teacher. What do you want to achieve this year?

Using coaching in the classroom

Coaching can also be practised every day in the classroom. Current teaching approaches include assessment for learning, blended learning, hybrid learning, collaborative learning, inquiry-based learning, metacognition and flipped classrooms.

Modern classrooms should also include coaching. The report *The Future of Skills: Employment in 2030* (Bakhshi et al, 2017) identified a skills gap in students entering the workforce, as well as the need to adapt educational approaches to meet the requirements of the rapidly evolving job market. The report highlighted the need to foster skills of creativity, critical thinking, collaboration and adaptability, and to instil the skills required for independent learning, vital to embrace new skill development in order to respond to changing career pathways. Rote learning of facts or a focus on the acquisition of knowledge are no longer as important as instilling the desire to learn, and the teaching of the skills required to learn independently. Teachers coaching pupils can help them to learn independently. Coaching can also help teachers become more motivated and take greater ownership of their own development.

The report from Bakhshi et al (2017) also highlighted how schools need to prepare students to adapt to new technologies. Since Amazon created Alexa in 2014, students have been fully aware how easy it is to find the answers to any questions they may pose. Even surfing the internet has come a long way since the 1996 search tool Ask Jeeves. The further development of artificial intelligence (AI) means coaching practices are required more than ever. As ChatGPT says:

> *AI-powered coaching, utilising tools like ChatGPT, has the potential to transform classrooms by enabling collaborative, personalised learning. Educators can engage students with real-time feedback and resources, promoting autonomy and critical thinking. AI insights help teachers adapt instruction, bridge gaps, and enhance the overall educational experience.*

The age-old adage 'What's the point of learning that?' is a common expression that questions the value or relevance of acquiring certain knowledge or skills. It reflects doubts about the practicality or applicability of what is being taught. This phrase often arises when individuals fail to see the immediate connection between what they are learning and its potential real-world application. However, it is important to recognise that education encompasses a broader purpose beyond immediate utility. Coaching can help pupils develop independence and autonomy as they apply their learning to real-world situations. Although one would hope that teachers do not see the futility of learning for their pupils, some teachers have an attitude of futility towards learning new content, adopting new curriculums or engaging in new use of technology, and may have an attitude of futility towards appraisal systems. This may have been indicative of a poor appraisal system, but it can also reflect a need to develop a love of learning for self-development in the teacher.

Learning encompasses personal growth, cognitive development, critical thinking and the acquisition of a wide range of knowledge and skills that can be beneficial in various contexts. While it is natural to seek understanding of the practical relevance of what is being learned, it is equally important to acknowledge the inherent value of learning for personal enrichment, intellectual curiosity, and long-term adaptability. Coaching approaches can help teachers and pupils to gain autonomy in setting their own achievable and relevant goals and help them on their individual pathways. A coaching approach is therefore also a useful tool for appraisals.

The integration of coaching in educational settings can be used by teachers with pupils but can also be transformative where teachers coach each other. Coaching can be used among staff for nurturing self-awareness, the development of a growth mindset and improving resilience, allowing staff to thrive. Coaching can be used for learning and development, raising performance or standards, or exploring attitudes and behaviour. Coaching builds relationships and develops teachers' growth, happiness and performance. We will explore some of these uses and look at practical examples, but the main focus of this book is on how the TEACHER coaching model can help to improve the teacher appraisal process, and help to develop a coaching culture.

Coaching versus mentoring

Coaching has evolved over the years, and so has mentoring. The difference between coaching and mentoring depends on the style of coaching and mentoring used, the formality and nature of the session, and the relationship between the individual and the person aiding their development. Some mentoring approaches can be very similar to coaching. Sketch et al (2001) state that mentoring used to be for executive high-flyers, and coaching for remedying poor performance. Both coaching and mentoring have changed and coaching should no longer have negative connotations of poor performance, as it is linked with growth and development – which applies to everyone, no matter how successful they, or others, think they are. Renton (2009) comments on a further distinction: how mentoring is often focused on careers and personal development, whereas coaching's purpose is usually on specific development areas. It can easily be argued that coaching, as it has developed, can be used for any of these purposes too.

The *Cambridge English Dictionary* has a traditional view when it describes mentoring as '*the act or process of helping and giving advice to a younger or less experienced person, especially in a job, or at school*'. This fixed description does not apply to coaching, as a coach does not have to be older or more experienced. It is not even a prerequisite that a teacher coach would need to know anything about teaching.

Renton (2009) writes about mentoring and reminds us of a quote from Anthony Robbins, the author of *Awaken the Giant Within*: '*If you want to be successful, find someone who achieved the results and copy what they do.*' Parsloe and Wray (2000, p 22) describe mentoring as being about encouraging *'people to manage their own learning in order that they may maximise their potential, develop their skills, improve their performance and become the person they want to be'*. In this definition, the blurred lines of coaching and mentoring are visible. They are both supportive and designed to help individuals develop, but coaching involves guidance for an individual to set their own goals and plan, whereas mentoring often has a more telling approach.

The word 'mentor' comes from Greek mythology. Odysseus trusted his good friend Mentor to protect and advise his son, Telemachus, when he left for the Trojan War. As with Mentor and Telemachus, a mentor is traditionally older, more knowledgeable and more experienced than their mentee, as shown in many descriptions of mentoring. This may be seen more often in a teacher–pupil relationship, but it can apply to coaching too. For teachers, mentoring may be more relevant at an early stage in a person's career so a more experienced mentor can share their knowledge and experience, but coaching can still be more effective.

Ragins and Cotton (1999) researched gender differences in mentoring. They looked at the work of Kram (1983) and mentor role theory, and found mentoring to have psychological functions, *'which contribute to the protégé's personal growth and professional development'* and career development functions *'which facilitate the protégé's advancement in the organisation'* (Ragins and Cotton, 1999, p 529). These included sponsoring job developments and promotions; coaching and protecting the protégé (maybe from a tricky parental email), providing challenging assignments and helping to raise the protégé's profile. For teaching staff, this might translate as advice on becoming a head of department, helping the mentee to set goals, helping them handle difficult parents, suggesting projects for development – for example, increased use of tracking of assessment data – and providing opportunities – for example, responsibility for running a school event. Coaching can also be used in all these instances. The outcomes of a successful coaching or mentoring relationship for an individual might include greater motivation, increased happiness and more job satisfaction, promotion, organisational commitment, financial gains and increased opportunities.

Formal and informal mentoring

Ragins and Cotton (1999) also researched formal and informal mentoring. Formal structured mentoring might be a planned session to discuss initial teacher training and progress, whereas informal mentoring might include advice on how to use Microsoft Teams, dispensed with coffee in hand while waiting for the photocopier. Their research showed that there was a place for both informal and formal mentoring, but that informal mentoring may be more effective than formal – particularly for women. Informal coaching between teachers can occur in many situations, such as teacher collaboration time, shared planning periods, subject department meetings, informal breaks, in teacher workrooms and as part of professional learning communities. These informal interactions provide opportunities for educators to exchange insights, discuss effective teaching strategies, share resources and collaborate on curriculum development. Additionally, teacher observation and feedback, mentoring relationships, co-teaching arrangements and discussions about student challenges, technology integration, parent communications and assessment methods contribute to a collaborative environment that supports teachers' professional growth (which hopefully then enhances student learning experiences). Just as the research showed for mentoring, in all of these informal coaching situations it may also be true that women prefer informal to formal coaching.

Informal and formal mentoring are not the only types of mentoring: peer mentoring, group mentoring and reverse (where the mentor is younger or less experienced mentor than the mentee) mentoring are other variations. Although the dictionary definition appears to contradict this, mentoring is often linked with older and more experienced mentors but it does not have to be. Germain (2008) states that mentoring and the provision of a safe environment can help people recognise their abilities and limitations. Just as a leader can help those in their team by imparting knowledge, skills or experience, a leader may also benefit from acquiring new skills from someone more junior. For instance, a younger teacher may mentor a head teacher and a director of studies in the use of virtual reality (VR) headsets. This has happened, and if you have not tried a VR headset be prepared to be mentored, or preferably coached, into strategies for coping with nausea while wearing it!

Renton (2009) quotes Elizabeth Coffey, who was awarded Mentor of the Year in 2007, said, *'A good mentor has wisdom, a low ego, and a determination to ensure that the person they're mentoring succeeds.'* These are also good qualities for a coach to have. Renton (2009) outlines how mentees do not need just one mentor but can have multiple mentors and can use them as a resource. She describes mentees as being able to acquire their own personal board of directors.

Coaching can also be formal or informal, to individuals or groups, and involve peer-coaching in addition to reverse coaching. In fact, pretty much everything great mentioned about mentoring applies to coaching too. Coaching can be used in so many areas across an individual's work and personal life. I am sure there would be benefits to gaining a personal board of director coaches too. The main difference between coaching and mentoring is the coach's or mentor's position on the spectrum of 'telling', or being directed what to do, and the autonomy, involvement and role of the coachee.

The coaching spectrum

There are numerous definitions of both coaching and mentoring, but Pearson (2016) forms the distinction by them being on a spectrum of helping that slides from very directive to non-directive. Mentoring can take a 'telling' approach, whereas coaching, according to Whitmore (2002, p 2), is a *'management behaviour that lies at the opposite end of the spectrum to command and control'*.

Tannenbaum and Schmidt's (1958) Continuum is a model of leadership that explains the same directive to non-directive spectrum approach. The model is a spectrum of helping from authority of the leader to freedom for the individual, and it moves from telling to selling, consulting, sharing and then delegating. Situational leadership follows this model with areas of delegating, participating, selling and telling as approaches of guidance that can be used in different situations. Schilder (2015) advocates the need for situational leadership, and the importance of choosing the right leadership style.

Mosston's Spectrum of Teaching Styles (Mosston and Ashworth, 1994) has much in common with these models. Coaching and mentoring in different forms can look very similar, but coaching includes a non-directive, less command-focused, less telling approach, and includes more freedom and individualisation for the coachee.

An experienced teacher will know when to use each of Mosston's teaching styles, or when to use synchronous or asynchronous learning, hybrid, virtual or blended learning, or flipped classrooms. In the same way, an experienced leader will be familiar with situational leadership and when different approaches may work best. An experienced teacher and leader should also know when coaching is the best tool. Even if it is group coaching, rather than the more common individual coaching, coaching is about personalisation and what is best for each unique team or individual.

There are many different models of coaching but, as a teacher, having a bespoke approach for coaching in an educational setting, focusing on the needs of both staff and pupils, is beneficial. The TEACHER model has been created for educational settings, and is based on knowledge gained from research into good practice in both coaching and mentoring. The TEACHER model is particularly useful as a tool for staff appraisals.

The TEACHER model

The TEACHER model can be used by staff with pupils, for staff peer coaching or for pupils with other pupils. The TEACHER model could also be used by pupils on staff for reverse coaching. The model can be used in a multitude of situations within an educational setting, and helps give structure to coaching conversations. The structure is particularly helpful for inexperienced coaches but can be used by inexperienced and experienced coaches alike.

The TEACHER acronym stands for the following:

- **T**arget;
- **E**nlightenment;
- **A**chievement;
- **C**hoice;
- **H**elp;
- **E**ncouragement;
- **R**eflection.

The components of the TEACHER model can be applied in school settings and has potential for increasing happiness and productivity. It can help to develop increased autonomy for individuals, promote a growth mindset and develop performance and increased well-being through goal-setting and action plans. It can also be used for learning and development, raising performance and standards or exploring attitudes and behaviours. The model will be explained in more detail in Chapter 4, but some uses are outlined below. The situations have been listed under a particular heading, but the entire TEACHER approach would be used.

Target

- Bringing a coaching approach to careers discussions, particularly when a pupil is not clear on their hopes for a future job.
- Coaching a teacher on how to make the most of a parents' meeting.
- Coaching pupils to help them find a subject for research for a project qualification.
- Coaching in appraisals and initial discussions to try to find areas for development.

Enlightenment

- Coaching using an instructional coaching approach where teachers use motion-sensitive cameras to film themselves using research-based teaching methods, instead of a lesson observation, and discuss feedback from the lesson.
- Coaching and the monitoring of marginal gains using an online platform for pupils for recording their skills development and achievements.
- Coaching on how to give and receive feedback and the development of a growth mindset.
- Coaching a new head and the use of 360 feedback.
- Coaching and feedback during a staff induction process.

Achievement

- Coaching and the use of personal development plans and Gantt-style charts for monitoring progress.
- Coaching pupils to deliver praise effectively when they buddy with younger pupils to hear them read.
- Celebrating staff achievements during an appraisal.

Choice

- Coaching and the discussion of options for conflict resolution when a pupil has received a sanction.
- Coaching pupils to deal with nerves when engaged in public speaking.
- Coaching in an Emotional Literacy Support Assistant (ELSA) session to help a pupil find resources or coping strategies to overcome challenges or manage difficult emotions.
- Coaching a teacher to consider options on their pathway to a management or leadership role.

Help

- Coaching during teacher training and helping to set SMART goals.
- Coaching of pupils in one-on-one situations and the creation of goals and development plans for the year ahead.
- Coaching pupils to create a plan for a group project based on each other's strengths and weaknesses.
- Coaching in an appraisal and the formation of a personal development plan.

Encouragement

- Coaching and the use of gamification for professional development within the Microsoft Learn training platform.
- Coaching pupils to support and encourage each other during groupwork.
- Coaching and the use of pupils as digital champions to coach and encourage their peers and staff and to encourage development and use of technology.

Reflection

- Coaching conversations at half-time on a hockey-pitch.
- Coaching to reflect on goals, progress, happiness, performance and future plans.

- Coaching conversations between staff during appraisals for addressing a better work–life balance.
- Group coaching on the impact of a coaching-based appraisal system, and plans for further improvements.

Applying the TEACHER model not only helps foster improved relationships with other people in the teaching community, but also helps to cultivate stronger relationships with learning and growth. Applying the TEACHER model helps promote happiness in the community and motivates everyone to greater performance and success.

The TEACHER model emphasises the building of positive relationships based on trust and encouragement, empowering people to take ownership of their education and development, and to exercise autonomy in setting goals and making choices. It promotes reflection and self-assessment to align plans and targets with personal growth and achievement. By fostering a growth mindset and unlocking potential through self-discovery, the model instils a lifelong desire for independent learning. It emphasises the benefits of feedback and creating an environment that supports happiness and a sense of empowerment, ultimately nurturing confident, self-directed individuals who are productive and well prepared for future success. The TEACHER model used in appraisals can help with encouraging goal-setting and alignment of goals, growth, development, relationship with feedback and reflection, and hopes to develop greater happiness and performance for teachers.

STAFF TRAINING DISCUSSIONS

- Where do you think your current appraisal system sits on a spectrum of directed to non-directed approaches?
- How could coaching be used for all professional development?

- What types of coaching do you think work best, and in which situations and with which people – formal or informal, individual or group?
- How could staff benefit from a TEACHER coaching approach to appraisals?

COACHING 'BOOK CLUB' SUGGESTIONS

Coaching for Performance: Growing People, Performance and Purpose by Sir John Whitmore. This is like a coaching bible; it is a super book in a simple-to-read style. This book introduces all the key coaching terms, lists coaching questions and has many helpful diagrams. If you only read one other coaching book, this should be it.

The Inner Game of Work: Overcoming Mental Obstacles for Maximum Performance by Timothy Gallwey. This book has many mini-models, including awareness, choice and trust triangles, and performance, learning and enjoyment triangles. The main reason for reading it is to learn about interference from inner voices and 'Self 1' and 'Self 2'. Gallwey has written a series of 'Inner Game' books and you may prefer to read *The Inner Game of Tennis*, *The Inner Game of Golf*, *The Inner Game of Music* or even *The Inner Game of Stress*. Most coaching books will discuss inner voices and external distractions in some form, and this is probably the best description. This book makes me consider shouting (even in encouragement) less when I am coaching on the sideline.

Coaching and Mentoring: What They Are and How to Make the Most of Them by Jane Renton. You should read this book to differentiate between coaching and mentoring and

→

learn more about key people in coaching. Jane Renton is a former presenter of BBC2's *Money Programme*, and her style of writing, and the topics she writes about, may make this book more suitable for a senior manager or leader who is considering the introduction of more coaching principles into a school.

Chapter 2:
A BRIEF HISTORY OF COACHING

> **LEARNING OBJECTIVES**
> - To help you understand how coaching has developed.
> - To introduce you to some different coaching models including GROW and instructional coaching.
> - To discuss how you might use the various coaching models.

Early coaching

The term 'coaching' has evolved from the word's early use in the 1830s as a verb for carrying students through exams to having multiple definitions from multiple models about unlocking potential and achieving goals. There will undoubtedly be models not listed here that will have shaped coaching as we know it today, but the models we discuss below have shaped the formation of the TEACHER model for use in schools. Huge apologies to the creators of the models not listed here, as I am sure they will have played their part too.

Coaching in the 1930s

The word 'coaching' as we know it today was not really in use in the 1930s. However, Dale Carnegie and his 1937 book *How to Win Friends and Influence People* was really ahead of its time (see Carnegie, 2023). It is one of the biggest selling books of all time, having sold over 30 million copies. If the whole book had been rewritten to focus on how the techniques would benefit the person the reader used the techniques with, rather than how they would benefit the reader, then this would have been a coaching manual, although as a self-improvement manual you could argue it could certainly be used for self-coaching. The book is a great read, littered with interesting stories backing up his 'principles' on different areas, including techniques for winning people to your way of thinking and being a leader. He also describes how to handle people and make them like you (hence the title), and how to encourage people, or to *'arouse in the other person an eager want'*. You really should read this book if you have not done so already.

Carnegie comments on leaders having humility, and their starting point being praise and appreciation for the other person. He advocates coaching through his recommendation of not using a telling, directive approach but rather choosing to *'ask questions instead of giving direct orders; let the other person save face'*. He highlights the importance of celebrating achievements and says to *'praise the slightest improvement and praise every improvement – be 'hearty in your approbation and lavish in your praise'* (Carnegie, 2023, p 54). He also comments on the importance of making goals achievable and trying to *'make the fault seem easy to correct; and make the other person happy about doing the thing you suggest.'* (Carnegie, 2023, p 278). Here he is straying away from coaching principles, as although having a plan in which the coachee is invested is important, the coach should not be suggesting what to do, but rather facilitating the individual's own solution.

One aspect of the TEACHER model is its focus on achievement and ensuring that achievements are celebrated, even when enlightenment of strengths and weaknesses has already been considered. Carnegie commented on psychologist B F Skinner's work and how it was *'proved through experiments that an animal rewarded for good behaviour will learn much more rapidly, and retain what it learns far more effectively than an animal punished for bad behaviour'* (Carnegie, 2023, p 28). If we are to be resilient and have a growth mindset and learn from our mistakes, it seems only fair that we should also be 'lavish in our praise' and celebrate achievements fully.

Coaching in the 1950s

The phrase 'management by objectives' (MBO) was first used by Peter Drucker, an Austrian-American management consultant, in his 1954 book entitled *The Practice of Management*. Drucker outlined five steps: setting a vision; translating the vision into organisational objectives and sharing with employees; setting objectives for individuals or key performance indicators; monitoring progress; and evaluating and rewarding progress. There are the coaching principles of goal-setting, actions and reviewing progress in place, but the focus is on management over personal and professional development. Although the model could be followed by applying coaching principles, it was not based around trusted relationships and one-on-one conversations.

The ideas of alignment of organisational objectives with individual objectives, or key performance indicators (KPIs), is important when using the TEACHER model for appraisals, for staff development or to help students work out what their goals should be. An appraisal should not solely be about improved performance but should focus on developing the individual and improving their well-being. Coaching for an appraisal, or other uses of coaching in schools, is about good conversations, which did not appear to be the emphasis of Drucker's work.

Coaching in the 1960s

Muska Mosston was born in Israel. He was a soccer player, a concert violinist, an educator, a professor and an author. He developed Mosston's Spectrum of Teaching Styles (Mosston and Ashworth, 1994). Although coaching is typically more personalised than a teacher delivering instructions to a group, and typically involves a collaborative relationship between a coach and the coachee, Mosston was aware of the need for different approaches with different people, and the benefits of autonomy for the learner. Guided discovery was one of the styles on his spectrum. Jerome Bruner was accredited with coining the term 'guided discovery', but the term follows the philosophy of Socrates (470–399 BCE). The Socratic method is a form of inquiry that uses questioning and dialogue to stimulate critical thinking, encourage self-reflection and facilitate the discovery of knowledge. If we consider a spectrum of approaches to conversations, Mosston's guided discovery and the Socratic method allow ownership for the coachee.

The TEACHER method uses guided discovery and Socratic questioning techniques of open-ended questioning, which can be used at many stages of the coaching conversation for gaining perspective, clarifying situations and reflection. What have you learned so far? What do you think about the TEACHER model so far? What are you hoping to achieve by reading this?

Coaching in the 1970s and the inner game

Timothy Gallwey is an American author and coach. He wrote a stream of books involving the inner game, and his first was entitled *The Inner Game of Tennis* (Gallwey, 1974).

In his books, Timothy Gallwey describes the 'inner game' and how the coach's role is to help the coachee to become more aware. He describes 'Self 1' and 'Self 2' as the conversations that occur in a person's head. Self 1 is the critic, and he describes better performance occurring when Self 1 is quiet and the cycle of interference has been broken. Personality types would affect the relationship between Self 1 and Self 2 and further to that,

Appleby (2022) writes that understanding personality types can help coaching for both the coach and coachee. The coach's role was not to offer solutions, but to help the coachee find *'non-judgemental awareness'* (Gallwey, 2000, p 10). Gallwey describes the technique of using transposing to try to consider what the other person is thinking and feeling.

Although Gallwey's early books were related to sport, as Gallwey himself was a tennis player, he found himself more often than not lecturing to businessmen and women rather than sportsmen and women. He wrote *The Inner Game of Work* in 1999, and *The Inner Game of Stress* in 2009.

Transposing can be practised using the TEACHER model. This can include shifting perspectives – for example, what would you say if you were talking to yourself now, and what would you say if an older version of you came and spoke to you? It can also include taking helicopter views; it could include discussing alternative scenarios and 'what if' style questions; reframing, role reversal and metaphorical questioning. If life is a journey, is coaching the compass that guides you to your desired destination? Is coaching, embodied by the TEACHER model, the compass that guides you like a skilled teacher and, just as a teacher imparts knowledge, does a coach help you to gain wisdom for your life's expedition?

Coaching in the 1980s

The CLEAR model and the GROW model

The CLEAR model was created in the 1980s by Peter Hawkins (2012). CLEAR stands for:

- **C**ontract;
- **L**isten;
- **E**xplore;
- **A**ction;
- **R**eview.

This model is similar to other coaching models in its exploration of the current situation and options, and the emphasis for the coach on listening. However, this model also mentions the importance of reflection and discusses the idea of contracting. The contracting stage is about clarifying goals, and defining roles and responsibilities. It is also about addressing logistics, setting expectations and establishing trust and confidentiality. For those familiar with Myers-Briggs, this model might appeal to those learners with a notion of feeling and doing, from it being action oriented and for the creation of a safe and supportive environment for the coaching conversation.

The GROW model was created by Sir John Whitmore, an author and British Racing Driver. I love the simplicity of Whitmore's model. GROW stands for:

- **G**oal;
- **R**eality;
- **O**ptions;
- **W**ill.

This is where the coach guides the coachee to set a goal, and through the will stage they commit to a plan. The reality stage is about assessing the current situation, exploring perspectives and identifying gaps. It is where the coach helps the coachee with perspective and self-awareness. With greater clarity about a situation and about their own strengths and weaknesses, coachees can develop greater self-awareness, leading to greater self-efficacy. According to Tieger, Barron and Tieger (2007) coachees may consider their strengths and consider roles they may be best suited for. Moen and Allgood (2009) looked at research from over 6000 published studies, and examined the relationship between people's confidence and their ability to reach their goals. They described self-efficacy as being *'(often the single most important factor) contributing to successful performances in almost every area of life'* (Moen and Allgood, 2009, p 71). The O of the GROW model is the options element;

it is about brainstorming, assessing, evaluating, selecting and prioritising options, and considering strategies for action. W is for will and commitment.

The CLEAR model is useful for the development of contracting. Using the TEACHER model for contracting, a visual activity might be to draw circles of disclosure diagrams, where there is an investigation of public and private boundaries for disclosure – that is, a visual representation of what you are happy to discuss. Whether you are using the TEACHER model with staff or with pupils, it is important to consider contracting. It is also important for the coachee to know who their thoughts might be shared with – possibly a head of department, a head or a head of human resources – and why this is necessary. It is helpful if the coach and coachee know how they are arranging meetings and where they are going to be held. Some coaches like to ask the coachee where they would feel comfortable, or even draw a picture of a suitable environment. Some coachees might even prefer a coaching walk, so they can experience some fresh air and the opportunity of no direct eye contact.

The GROW model is a super model for its simplicity, which might appeal to pragmatists; however, the TEACHER model adds a little more structure to coaching conversations – which provides a particular benefit to those who are new to coaching. Although it is not necessary to follow TEACHER in order, the letters can be thought of as being like the subheadings of a lesson plan to provide a guide for a coaching conversation.

Coaching in the 1990s

Coach U and the Co-active coaching model

The Co-active model was created by Kimsey-House, Kimsey-House, Sandahl and Whitworth (2011). It is a star-shaped model with four cornerstones and with listening, intuition, curiosity, self-management and deepening/forwarding at its pinnacles, all centred around fulfilment, balance and purpose. Four areas surround this model: the first area is to *'evoke transformation'*, the second is to *'focus on the whole person'*, the third is to *'dance in this moment'* and the fourth is to *'be naturally creative, resourceful and whole'* (Kimsey-House et al, 2011, p 8). The coach would apply this model to elicit the values that people hold, and to actively listen so they could engage in all aspects of conversations, even when they go off track slightly – hence dancing in the moment. This model encourages the coachee to take ownership and to realise that when they are open and really listen, they can find their own answers.

I think I probably lost you at 'star-shaped model'. This really is a great book that is well worth reading, but the intricacies might be a little tricky to explain to a Year 6 pupil or a teacher who is new to coaching if you were trying to help them use a model. The TEACHER model has sufficient simplicity and structure to help novice coaches uses coaching principles too. As in the Co-active model, the focus on the whole person in TEACHER coaching is important, as this is the link for work–life balance, or the link between pastoral and academic development.

The Co-active coaching model was developed in the 1990s, the same decade that Coach U was founded. Coach U was founded by Thomas Leonard, who was also instrumental in the founding of the International Coach Federation, and the International Association of Coaching. Leonard founded Coach U, a virtual university, in 1992. There are many different types of coaching, including executive coaching, relationship coaching, academic coaching, performance coaching and life coaching. One model for executive coaching is integrative coaching, which describes six streams or levels of coaching (Passmore, 2007). This model was developed for executive coaching and might not apply to life coaching, or other coaching types. Thomas Leonard is sometimes referred to as the founder of life coaching. He was an American financial adviser who applied the financial coaching principles he was using to life coaching. He wrote *The Portable Coach: 28*

Sure-fire Strategies for Business and Personal Success (Leonard, 1998), which outlines 28 attraction principles. These include creating a vacuum that pulls you forward, as he comments that being pulled forward is attractive, while pushing forward is not.

The ethos of coaching, and its reliance on good conversations, was summed up by Leonard, who said that all problems exist in the absence of good conversation. The principle of good conversations is instrumental to the effective use of the TEACHER model. However, Leonard's work focuses on life coaching. The TEACHER model can be used for life coaching, but it can also be used for improving happiness and performance, and is designed for use in educational settings.

Coaching in the 2000s

OSCAR, ACHIEVE, T-GROW, STEPPA and Instructional Coaching models

The 2000s saw many further coaching models being developed. Confusingly, in 2002, two similar models, OSCAR and OSKAR, were created. The OSKAR model was created by McKergow and Jackson (2002) and stands for: Outcome, Scaling, Know-How, Affirm and Action, and Review. The Outcome element involves discussing goals and the Know-how consists of discussing options. The affirm and action is about plans and progress. One important element to this model is scaling. This is using scaling techniques – for example, on a scale of 1–10, how close to 10 are you on achieving your goal?

The OSCAR coaching model by Gilbert and Whittleworth (2009) stands for: Outcome, Situation, Choices, Action and Review. Of the two OSCAR/OSKAR models, this is my favourite as I like its simplicity. It is very similar to the GROW model: whether it is Goal or Outcome, Reality or Situation, Options or Choices, or Will or Action does not matter. The further development that the OSCAR has on the GROW model is its reference to the coaching cycle through the R for Review, and the stress on the importance of checking progress. The TEACHER model has many similarities to these two models. Target replaces goals and outcomes, Enlightenment replaces Situation and Reality, Choice replaces Options, and Help focus goals substitutes for Will and Action. The OSCAR and TEACHER models both encourage Review or Reflection.

The TEACHER model builds further on OSCAR and OSKAR. OSKAR scaling techniques can be used as part of any TEACHER coaching conversation when discussing goals, choices and commitment to plans. The TEACHER model also adds to the enlightenment, reality or discussion of situation stages of the conversation by building on conversations around strengths and weaknesses and perspectives, and ensuring there is also sufficient emphasis on celebrating the achievements of the coachee.

In 2003, three further important coaching models were created: T-GROW, STEPPA and ACHIEVE. The T-GROW model was created by Miles Downey (2002). It builds on the GROW model, with the addition of T for Topic. I think this model represents a shift in the use of coaching principles. As explained earlier, coaching and mentoring have both evolved, and coaching was once linked to shorter-term relationships, and coaching for a specific skill or objective. The evolution of coaching principles has meant that they can now be applied in a much wider range of areas. The Topic element of the T-GROW model allows for the bigger picture, broader area or wider environment to be discussed, and helps the coach and coachee develop their relationship and gain greater understanding about the purpose of their conversations.

One barrier to personal development can be resistance to change. The Stages of Change (or Transtheoretical) model was developed by Prochaska and DiClemente (1983). The stages are described as pre-contemplation, contemplation, preparation, action and maintenance. It might be easiest to consider the stages in the context of a goal such as dieting, with pre-contemplation being when you first start thinking about it. The T-GROW model considers these barriers, as the coach and coachee discuss the topic, and then moves through perspective, the reality of the need to change – that is, contemplating the changes – setting goals and discussing options – that is, preparing to change – and then planning the way forward through a solid commitment to action and maintenance.

T-GROW is another favourite model. If feedback and gaining perspective on the reality of situations are elements of coaching, then it is possible that if the coaching conversation starts with the goal or the outcome, the whole purpose of the conversation may head in the wrong direction. An example might be using coaching as part of an appraisal system. If the coachee starts the conversation with their goals before discussing feedback on their performance, then they may later need to alter their goals once they have greater clarity about their situation. The Topic element allows for the bigger picture to be discussed; specific goals are discussed later. The TEACHER coaching model embraces this approach, with the Target stage being a discussion of aims for the sessions and a discussion of potential goals and objectives, before feedback helps to shape the goals, followed later by the honing of those goals and the creation of a plan.

The 2003 STEPPPA (or STEPPA – sometimes one of the Ps is left out) model, created by McLeod (2003), stands for Subject, Target, Emotions, Perception, Plan, Pace and Action. As with the TEACHER and T-GROW models, this model separates the subject from the goal (Target in this case). The STEPPPA model also looks at factors affecting the reality or perspective of a situation, splits the wider context from the emotional context, and recognises and values the emotions of the coachee.

The ACHIEVE model was also created in 2003. The ACHIEVE coaching model was developed by Eldridge and Dembkowski (2004) and was also built on the foundations of the GROW coaching model. Coach 4 Growth (2022) clearly explain the ACHIEVE model on their website, where they provide leadership tools, and outline coaching models. The coaching cycle of the ACHIEVE model is a seven-stage process. The first stage is to 'Assess the current situation'. At this stage in the cycle, the coach and coachee are building their relationship. Through active listening, the coach helps the coachee to discuss their current situation before moving on to the next stage in the coaching cycle, 'Creative brainstorming', where options for moving forward are discussed. The third and fourth stages are 'Hone the goals' and 'Initiate option generation'. The coach then helps the coachee to 'Evaluate options' and, when the goal is determined, to initiate 'Valid action programme design' before deciding the next steps. Throughout the coaching cycle, the coach has a role to motivate and 'Encourage momentum' and commitment to achieving the goal. The balance of input from the coach and the coachee may vary throughout the different stages of the cycle.

The ACHIEVE model has also highly influenced the TEACHER model. Again, the similarities lie in the separation of the Target or the assessment of the situation, from the honing of the actual goal. The TEACHER model, like the ACHIEVE model, also focuses on the role of the coach in addressing the importance of encouragement and motivation, and ensuring commitment to goals.

The actual year of creation of the WOOP coaching model is unclear. The model of Wish, Outcome, Obstacle and Plan was developed by Oettingen (2014), who is a German princess and a professor. According to the WOOP website, it is *'usually examined under the scientific term Mental Contrasting with Implementation Intentions, abbreviated MCII'* and is about mentally contrasting the future with the current situation. This contrasting element is of particular importance as Oettingen's research showed that positive thinking and visualising goals was not enough, and considering the potential obstacles was important too, as otherwise the goals were less likely to be realised. Her model also considered the Wish or the goal and then further explored the idea of an 'Outcome' and thinking about the imagery of the goal, and what it would look and feel like to achieve this goal. Buddha apparently had the same thoughts: *'What you think, you become. What you feel, you attract. What you imagine, you create.'*

The final area of coaching to be discussed is instructional coaching, although I would define this as a practice rather than a model. Instructional coaching was developed by Jim Knight. He defines instructional coaches as *'individuals who are full-time professional developers, on-site in schools. Instructional coaches work with teachers to help them incorporate research-based instructional practices ... that respond directly to teachers' burning issues'* (Knight, 2007, p 17). Knight outlines the main areas as relating to what he calls the big four: behaviour of pupils, content knowledge, direct instruction and formative assessment. He outlines seven principles as the theoretical foundation of instructional coaching: Equality, Choice, Voice, Dialogue, Reflection, Praxis and Reciprocity. Knight explains that 'Voice' concerns helping the coachee to find the words to say what matters to them and 'Praxis' is about learning where knowledge can be recreated so it can be used in personal and professional lives. Knight also comments on the spiral model of change, which builds on the Stages of Change model. He writes that people can move through different stages in a change model, but they do not always do this in a linear fashion.

If you are applying the TEACHER coaching model for staff appraisals, then I would thoroughly recommend Jim Knight's book. There are some further interesting points including the use of self-reflection and filming of lessons. Instructional coaching also puts an emphasis on teacher development through the use of dedicated instructional coaches. This use of resources is not something that is often seen in British schools, but it helps to drive a coaching culture. Instructional coaching principles could easily be used alongside the TEACHER model.

Coaching in the 2010s

The FUEL coaching model

Hopefully you have now understood how models have developed and can consider the context of their development. The 1990s saw a surge in interest in self-improvement and personal development, with books and seminars on leadership, motivation and success becoming popular. There was also a shift from remedial to developmental coaching. Coaching had previously been used to address performance issues. However, in the late twentieth century there was a shift towards using coaching as a proactive and developmental tool to foster growth and excellence. The number of coaching models created to reflect this changing landscape is not surprising.

The FUEL coaching model was created by Zenger and Stinnett (2010). FUEL stands for:

- **F**rame conversation;
- **U**nderstand current state;
- **E**xplore;
- **L**ay out success plan.

This model also reflects changes in coaching practice, where the starting point is not necessarily a predetermined goal, and the nature of the relationship and the conversation is discussed before trying to understand the current state of the coachee. Zenger and Stinnett (2010) provide further discussion stimuli to develop under each of the headings of their model. Under 'Frame Conversation', these include identifying the behaviour or issue to discuss, determining the purpose of the conversation and agreeing on the process for the conversation. Other useful conversation stimuli are provided for the vision for success through considering performance expectations, exploring alternative paths of action and exploring possible barriers or resistance.

The FUEL model lists a detailed set of questions that really help to ensure that a coaching approach is about relationships and having helpful conversations. The TEACHER model builds on the principles behind the FUEL model, with more emphasis on reflection.

All the models outlined above have helped to shape the TEACHER coaching model, which is designed specifically for use in educational environments.

Coaching in the 2020s

The TEACHER coaching model

Why use the TEACHER approach? The TEACHER model has been created to enable a simple framework for coaching conversations that can be used by teachers and students alike, and for coaching others or personal development. The TEACHER model is designed to encourage performance gains and increase happiness, and is particularly useful as a model for staff appraisals. The model helps to foster a culture based on relationships and growth mindsets, empowering individuals to embrace autonomy and envision personal development. TEACHER describes 'Target', 'Enlightenment', 'Achievement', 'Choice', 'Help', 'Encouragement' and 'Reflection'.

The 'Target' element is about targets and starting to focus on goals. This stage involves establishing the relationship, building trust and rapport, contracting boundaries on what can be shared and with whom, exploring possible areas for growth and starting to focus on goals, and discussing what good coaching conversations and outcomes look like.

'Enlightenment' is about considering different perspectives and the reality of situations. This is the stage where motivations will be discussed and feedback will be shared on actions, skills, knowledge, attitudes, behaviours and emotions. Strengths and weaknesses of the coachee will be explored. This is the stage where perspective will be considered and the reality of situations will be discussed.

The 'Achievement' stage of the model focuses on recognition and celebration of achievements. This stage is about ensuring that achievements are noticed, recorded and celebrated.

The 'Choice' stage is about continuing to explore a choice of goal and options for achieving goals.

The 'Help' stage is where the coachee is helped to form and refine their goals and form plans of action. This is the stage where goals will become SMART goals and a plan for the achievement of the goals is created, which allows for progress to be monitored, and marginal gains and milestones to be recognised.

The 'Encouragement' stage is about encouragement and motivation, and ensuring the coachee remains motivated and supported as they move closer to achieving their goal. This stage is about discussion of motivation during the goal-setting stage and motivation to action the goal. It involves the coach providing encouragement and support, and the coachee recognising the importance of self-motivation.

The final stage is the 'Reflection' stage; this involves reflection on progress, and reviewing and improving goals when necessary. It also involves reflection after achieving the goal to gain awareness of lessons learned before embarking further on the coaching cycle and setting future goals.

Using the TEACHER model correctly requires appreciating that it is a coaching model in which part of the discovery is finding the correct goal. Further to identifying strengths and weaknesses, time is taken to note and celebrate achievements, and reflection is important and is part of the coaching cycle.

STAFF TRAINING DISCUSSIONS

- What do you think makes a good conversation on goals?
- What helpful advice would you give yourself if you could travel back in time? Are there any patterns in the types of advice people would give to themselves?
- Do you think staff are praised regularly enough, and do you think staff are happier and more motivated to work hard if they are praised? Explain your answer.
- How do you set a goal before you are self-aware of your own performance? If not, what could you do before setting a goal or goals?

COACHING 'BOOK CLUB' SUGGESTIONS

Co-active Coaching: Changing Business Transforming Lives by Henry Kimsey-House, Karen Kimsey-House, Phillip Sandahl and Laura Whitworth. I would suggest reading this once you have a basic understanding of coaching. It has lots of sample dialogue and some excellent exercises. Many tools and techniques are described, which may be a bit overwhelming for a beginner coach, but this book is definitely worth a read when you have practised more and need more ideas.

Instructional Coaching: A Partnership Approach to Improving Instruction by Jim Knight. This book introduces instructional coaching, which is where teachers are coached to use research-based practice. It involves an instructional coach who operates in a school supporting professional development. Instructional coaching features in many American schools and has been around since 2007. The term is gaining recognition in the UK, and this book will

→

explain more. Even if a school does not appoint someone to operate solely as an instructional coach, it contains some great ideas that could be used for professional development in schools. Instructional coaching courses are also available.

How to Win Friends and Influence People by Dale Carnegie. This really is a great read. It is full of quotes, examples and principles to live your life by, including rules for making your home life happier and how not to dig a 'marital grave' – although apparently you need to buy an early edition to get this part! I can't believe I only read this in 2023, and I wish I had read it earlier.

Chapter 3:
THE CASE FOR COACHING

LEARNING OBJECTIVES

- To help you recognise the importance of a growth mindset, collaboration, alignment of individual goals with organisational goals.
- To enable you to realise how these things can help bring about greater happiness and performance improvements.
- To help you understand what a coaching culture is, and what its benefits might be.

'Built to last'

Built to Last: Successful Habits of Visionary Companies (Collins and Porras, 2004) examines 18 exceptional and long-lasting companies to try to extract a formula for success. According to the World Economic Forum, the average lifespan of multinational organisations is approximately 50 years. Successful organisations achieve success within a changing landscape. Collins and Porras write about clock-builders and time-tellers, and how it is more amazing to build a clock that tells the time forever than to have someone who is amazing at telling the time. They write that *'building a company that can prosper far beyond the presence of any single leader and through multiple product life cycles is clock-building'* (Collins and Porras, 2004, p 23).

For schools as organisations, you may be thinking survival is not as relevant unless you are considering an independent school in a changing political and financial climate, a failing school or a small village primary school struggling with low numbers. However, it is important to consider education more broadly in addition to specific institutions. Technological advances have had a big impact on schooling, and the future of education needs to also address the skills gap reported in our workforce. If educational institutions are to be clock-builders producing excellent teachers and successful students, they need to develop independence in their learners, and to instil a love of learning and an intrinsic desire for growth and development. Pupils today have knowledge at their fingertips. The internet, the development of smart assistants such as Cortana, Alexa or Siri, and the development of AI platforms such as ChatGPT have changed the landscape. Wanting to learn is arguably more important for students than what they learn. Ownership of learning and motivation to learn can be developed through the creation of a coaching culture, adopted by both staff and students. Staff who are being developed though coaching can help encourage independent learners and the growth of a coaching culture. Coaching should have a greater presence in schools.

A coaching culture

A coaching culture is about developing an organisation based on people and relationships, and unlocking potential. Morrison McGill (2017, p 163) discusses lesson grading and lesson observations, and states that, *'instead of all this nonsense – allow every teacher to be coached'*.

The Hudson Institute (2018), a research organisation promoting leadership in America, believes that culture shapes behaviours inside the organisation and that a coaching culture is one deliberately focused on growing and nurturing talent in order to deliver key results, strengthen leadership capacities, increase retention and deepen engagement. A coaching culture is based on feedback, learning and development.

Crane (2012, p 40) believes a *'true coaching culture is where feedback and coaching flow up, down and sideways, between people, their peers, and their managers'*. He comments on research on coaching cultures, and notes that people are now looking for intrinsic motivation and purpose at work. They want organisations with a clear vision and support that helps them feel appreciated and purposeful. Students and teachers alike spend more time in schools than they do at home, so finding purpose while at school is important. If coaching is for appraisals and you are considering purpose, try imagining a see-saw with purpose balanced on top, with work at one end and home on the other, and a fulcrum that can move. If coaching is for appraisals, it needs to be sufficiently regular to allow for changes in the balance of our purpose, and to give a coachee perspective on their purpose.

Executive coach Funck (2023) explains how a coaching culture *'improves not only the way employees interact with each other, but also the interactions they have with customers and potential clients'* through the building of *'conversational and coaching skills'*.

In educational establishments, the development of a coaching culture means that all staff and pupils recognise the importance of learning and development, and are open to feedback. Their attitudes to development have a wider effect on others in their community. Panagiotis, Sahinidis and Polychronopoulos (2015) also explain that creating motivational conditions, as in a coaching culture, makes the most of a work force. Pascale and Sternin (2005) discuss how certain individuals can be, what they describe as, positive deviants and sparkling exceptions who help improve the culture of learning and development.

Hawkins (2012) describes a detailed seven-step approach to developing a coaching culture, including developing a strategy and ensuring coaching includes performance management, ensuring support from leaders, developing coaches and embedding coaching, and making coaching the predominant management style. He comments on the need to embed feedback at every step of the coaching culture journey.

If coaching is fully embraced by educational institutions, staff and students, it needs to be practised by all stakeholders, including leaders and including during staff appraisals. Staff and students need to value feedback and the desire to grow and develop. As stated by Lundy and Cowling (1996), *'culture is the way we do things around here'*. It can be really tricky to take feedback onboard, whether it is feedback on how to improve something you are really proud of, or something you believe you are failing at. The more you embrace feedback, the easier it becomes, and the more you grow and develop.

Learning organisations

With increased globalisation and technology, organisations have to be flexible and willing to change and develop in order to succeed. If an organisation is focused on growing and developing, it can be considered a learning organisation.

Pedler, Burgoyne and Boydell (1997) describe a learning organisation as one that transforms through going through a life-cycle of stages and in which learning is available to all. A learning organisation *'facilitates the learning of all its members and continuously transforms itself'* (Pedler, Burgoyne and Boydell, 1997, p 1).

Peter Senge (1997) explores the characteristics and principles of learning organisations, which include systems thinking. In a school, systems thinking occurs when every part of the system is reviewed with everyone working towards providing excellent education. Senge also describes personal mastery, which involves individuals continuously developing their skills, competencies and mental models (an individual's assumptions and beliefs). He looks at the importance of developing a shared vision that aligns the efforts of all members of the organisation towards a common purpose, along with team learning and the importance of collaboration. Senge argues that a learning organisation is one that can learn not just from individual experiences but from its own experiences as a whole.

The central concept in Senge's work is that learning organisations continuously learn, adapt and improve. They foster a culture of learning and innovation, and their members are empowered to contribute their ideas and take risks in pursuit of organisational goals. An example of this is 'pupil voice' and pupils' empowerment to drive change in a learning organisation.

If educational institutions are 'built to last', they need to be 'learning organisations' where 'coaching cultures' are established, growth and development are embraced and failure is not feared. Creating a culture of coaching where people are open to feedback and an intrinsic desire to learn can help to improve performance and develop motivation and well-being within an organisation.

The growth mindset

A successful learning organisation and coaching culture depend on positive attitudes to learning, and the ability to develop a growth mindset. If you work in a school, or have children who go to school, you may well have been introduced to Carol Dweck's book *Mindset: Changing The Way You Think to Fulfil Your Potential*. Professor Dweck discusses attitudes to failure and encourages people to embrace failure as a way of developing and learning. She compares fixed and growth mindsets, and suggests that people with a fixed mindset believe their intellectual abilities are set from birth, or 'fixed', whereas those with a growth mindset believe they can grow their abilities. However, she does not suggest the improvement in ability comes without a commitment to hard work. I have worked at a school where we had training on growth mindset and were even given sparkly wands with the word 'Yet' on them, which we could brandish if we were told by anyone they could not do something, and enforce the growth mindset message that they could just not do it *yet*.

To develop a growth mindset, you need to have a good relationship with failure. Dr Goldman, a physician from Toronto, talks about the fear culture in medicine. He describes a baseball batter as having a batting average of 400 and only hitting the ball four times out of ten but this being deemed legendary while patients are not keen to see doctors boasting of similar success rates. Matthew Syed (2016) writes about this in *Black Box Thinking: Marginal Gains and the Secrets of High Performance.* He explains how everyone has the potential to improve, and how they need the right mindset to do so. Syed comments on the relationship the aviation industry has with failure, and it is used for growth. He describes how the black box (which is in fact orange) is used in aviation to record flight data, and can record sound and voices from the cockpit. If an aircraft crashes, the black box can be analysed to help with investigations, and to drive development and improvements. Feedback drives improvement.

Elizabeth Day (2019) writes about failure in her honest and humorous book *How to Fail*. She describes occasions in all areas of her life where she has failed, and how she learned from her mistakes, or redefined her own successes and failures. She also writes about the difference between failing and being a failure, and quotes Tim Harkness (sports scientist at Chelsea FC) who said, *'Losing is not a reflection of your potential or on your value as a person'* (Day, 2019, p 77).

Day (2019, p 224) writes further on failure and success, and how success only *'feels good when it is congruent with your personality'*. She discusses how something being deemed a success or failure can be based on opinion, and how important it is to own your goals and to consider your own definition of success. She illustrates this through her interview with actor Simon Pegg, who said:

> *You could be living on a rock in the middle of the ocean, wearing a pair of Y fronts, with a never-ending supply of sandwiches. If that makes you happy, then you're a complete success.*
>
> (Day, 2019, p 214)

Successful educational environments develop a coaching culture where people are not afraid to learn from their mistakes and are able to improve though setting goals.

Benefits to an organisation

Embedding a coaching culture within an organisation can have a multitude of benefits at the organisational level. These include effects related to performance and happiness.

Whitmore (2002, p 97) defines performance from coaching and real performance as *'going beyond what is expected, setting ones' own highest standard, invariably standards that surpass what others demand or expect'*. With regard to performance, organisational benefits include improved skills and abilities, leading to increased productivity; enhanced leadership skills; identifying and retaining talent; and goal alignment. Coaching ensures that individual goals align with organisational objectives, resulting in focused efforts and improved performance, and it also promotes continuous improvement and personal growth, contributing to a culture of learning and adaptability within the organisation. Through fostering a culture where failure is not feared, coaching promotes innovation and encourages creative thinking, leading to process improvements and innovative solutions to challenges.

Coaching can benefit productivity and performance management. The coach helps the coachee to ensure that their goals are aligned with the organisational goals, and to help them gain perspective and find options to succeed. The coach can ensure that an under-performing employee is fulfilling their role and can help challenge a motivated, productive employee to be more empowered and strive for greater success. Coaching aims to improve autonomy and independence, and helps individuals adapt to new challenges and responsibilities.

With respect to happiness, a coaching culture helps improve happiness and well-being; it helps people cope with stress, conflict and change management; and it helps build healthier relationships through its emphasis on communication and support. Coaching can help well-being and be more than just a *'sticky plaster solution'* (Morrison McGill, 2017, p 175). Coaching can help improve work–life balance, improve overall well-being and job satisfaction, and facilitate personal development, leading to increased self-awareness and fulfilment. Although this relates to personal well-being, coaching creates more motivated and productive employees and the organisation is therefore more likely to reach its performance targets.

In educational settings this means a coaching culture can help foster happier, more motivated and more effective and productive staff, as well as happier, motivated, more effective learners.

Happiness

A coaching culture can increase motivation, leading to developments and performance improvements. It is built on the foundations of establishing good relationships, growth mindsets and goals. Using feedback as a tool for learning means that developments can be made in attitudes and behaviours, performance and standards, and in the relationship with learning and development. This can lead to both personal and organisational gains, which feed back into the coaching cycle through increasing performance and happiness.

Shawn Achor (2011, p 4) writes about how *'waiting to be happy limits our brain's potential for success, whereas cultivating positive brains makes us more motivated, efficient, resilient, creative, and productive, which drives performance upward'*. If performance, motivation and happiness are interrelated in a coaching culture, then it is important to consider what happiness is.

Lee et al (2013) conducted research on happiness using a Peace of Mind Scale. Their findings were published in the wonderfully titled *Journal of Happiness Studies.* The reason for the establishment of this scale was to account for different cultures' interpretations of happiness. The World Happiness Report comments on global rankings, with Nordic countries often appearing at the top of the table (Sustainable Developments Solutions Network, 2023). Different nations have different views on happiness and whether it relates to comfort, peace, harmony, purpose, fulfilment, connectnedness, pleasure or excitement. We all have our own ideas of happiness, our emotional state after feeling the benefits of various hormones – including dopamine (the feel-good hormone), oxytocin (the love hormone) and serotonin (the mood regulating hormone) – linking our thoughts and feelings. It might be helpful in the first stages of a coaching conversation to ask a coachee what makes them happy.

Organisations have a requirement to consider staff welfare, and schools have the same obligation to consider pupil welfare. Although the terms 'well-being', 'happiness' and 'welfare' are often used interchangeably, welfare is defined as being physical and mental health and happiness, and well-being as health and happiness. *'Well-being allows us to consider a 'fully rounded humanity' whereas welfare focuses on economic utility'* (Taylor, 2011, p 778). An organisation can try to judge the health and happiness of its employees, but welfare and well-being are subjective. Subjective well-being is explained as being composed of cognitive and affective components. The cognitive element is the subject's life satisfaction and the affective element is their positive feelings and moods (Luhmann 2017). A person may or may not have happy things happening to them, but they can also choose whether or not to be happy. Subjective well-being can include a person's happiness, health, moods and feelings, and their life and job satisfaction.

Eudaimonia, the Greek word for happiness, welfare and spirit, was discussed by Aristotle, who is quoted as saying, *'Happiness is the meaning and purpose of life, the whole aim and end of human existence.'* Bryson, Forth and Stokes (2014) tried to pull all these terms together in their well-being model, where three areas link to workplace happiness and well-being: our affect, our job satisfaction and eudaimonia. Robertson and Cooper (2011), in *Well-being: Productivity and Happiness at Work*, examine how well-being can have both eudemonic and hedonistic aspects. The hedonistic aspect is our instances of happiness and how we recognise them. The eudemonic aspects include our self-acceptance, our relationships, our personal growth and our purpose in life.

Understanding happiness can be quite confusing, but it is crucial to remember that each of us has unique points of reference for happiness. Our environments, experiences of pleasure and joy, perceptions of happiness and its significance in fulfilling our meaning and purpose all differ from person to person. In a school or educational setting, we need to consider how happiness depends on the individual and is influenced by their age, gender, personality, values and social circumstances. Happiness will also depend on the environment and the work. Even if all these variables were the same for each individual, people would have their own peace of mind scale and perceive situations differently.

Research by Bryson, Forth and Stokes (2014) showed that happiness, or satisfaction, among employees in the workplace was positively correlated with productivity. A further study of 713 individuals by Oswald, Proto and Sgroi (2015) proved that happiness caused at least a 10 per cent increase in productivity.

A happier workforce brings numerous benefits to an organisation. Happier employees are more productive, more engaged and more likely to perform better, leading to improved overall productivity and job performance. A happier workforce also helps with staff retention, reducing turnover costs. A positive work environment fosters creativity, innovation and collaboration among employees. Additionally, happier employees provide better customer service, experience reduced absenteeism and contribute to a positive company culture. Prioritising employee happiness creates a healthier and more supportive work environment, enhancing employee well-being and overall organisational success.

Embedding a coaching culture in schools could create greater happiness for staff and students and have the secondary effect of creating happier parents. Focusing on happiness through emphasising relationships, and the increased autonomy, motivation and support offered through coaching, can lead to greater success for individuals and for the organisation as a whole.

Embedding a coaching culture can create a happier and more successful learning institution. The emphasis on trust and relationships can help to develop collaboration and community spirit, and allow for improved group, form, team or school, college or university experiences.

Collaboration and teams

A coaching culture means relationships are improved through greater trust and communication skills being developed within teams. In an educational setting, teams may refer to students or staff and types of teams may include sets, forms, sports teams, choirs, group work for projects, departments or senior management teams.

Different team types also include strategic, cross-functional or temporary teams. Regardless, the purpose of teams within an organisation is to help achieve a shared vision. Good working relationships can help teams to meet goals and targets more easily. However, one team member's actions and behaviours can impact the success or failure of the entire team. Team members may not feel valued or appreciated. If working relationships are ineffective, there may be limited trust within teams. Without trust, then effective collaboration is not possible and information cannot be shared easily. Conflict may be more likely to arise, leading to lower morale and feelings of negativity. Eleisha Training provide a range of coaching articles on their website, including a 2014 article on building trust (Eleisha Training, 2014). Teams can try and build their trust.

Effective teams are productive and foster positive relationships. People working in an effective team are clear on lines of communication, including what to communicate and with whom. Effective teams are built on mutual trust and respect. From his research on team productivity, Dr Meredith Belbin found that team cohesiveness affected productivity. He identified nine roles in an effective team: chair, shaper, implementer, complete-finisher, coordinator, resource investigator, thought-oriented plant, monitor-evaluator and specialist. He found that strong teams fulfilled each of these roles even if a person assumed more than one role. A coach may try to help a coachee consider which role or roles they fulfil. They may also coach to help a coachee consider the strengths of others and the roles they fulfil.

Effective teams help organisations to achieve their goals through good communication, playing to the strengths of team members, and establishing efficient and more productive working relationships with all stakeholders. Individuals can benefit from effective teamwork as they may feel proud to be part of a team through working in a supportive and secure environment where they benefit from the strengths of others while feeling that their own strengths are also recognised and valued.

Whether they are student or staff teams, teams can be coached to be more effective. One area with which coaching could help is in assisting team members to cope with the five stages of team development and behaviour. A model of team behaviour was outlined by Bruce Tuckman (1965). He described the stages of team relationships as forming, storming, norming and performing. His model was later adapted to include the fifth stage of adjourning or transforming. The forming stage is where the team members rely on their leader. The team are newly formed and are at the stage where they are establishing relationships and so may be polite or anxious. The second stage is storming. At this stage, frustrations are evident within the team. The team members have not acknowledged their roles and are competing with each other. During the norming stage, team members are aware of and accept their roles and responsibilities. There is a safer environment, where strengths and weaknesses can be acknowledged and respect is developing between the team members and between them and the leader. Following this comes the performing stage, where the team is working productively and efficiently, through respect and empowerment, as the leader is happier to delegate. A coaching culture can help teams through these stages as members communicate, give and receive feedback, reflect on their strengths and weaknesses, and set goals. According to Sandahl (2020), the benefits of team coaching can be improved team dynamics and better business metrics that matter to the team. Increased self-awareness is another benefit as members recognise their value and that of others. Bob Chapman (2013) of global capital equipment and engineering solutions company Barry-Wehmiller extols the virtues of getting the best out of a team. He maintains that organisations need to capture the gifts and talents of their staff and focus on optimising their value.

In a school, coaching for improved team performance can be introduced in many areas. Pupils could be coached to work more effectively in teams when they work in groups. Coaching can help pupils accept feedback and gain perspective on their strengths and weaknesses. Coaching for team performance can also be used by staff to hold more effective meetings. Managers could also be group coached to lead appraisal systems more effectively.

Coaching is closely linked to team learning and can significantly enhance the learning process within a team. A coaching culture supports team learning and helps increase happiness and performance.

Team learning

Senge (1997, p 236) believes *'team learning is the process of aligning and developing the capability of a team to create the results its members truly desire'* (Senge, 1997, p 236). He defines a learning organisation as one that is continually expanding its capacity to create its future, and compares the role of leaders in a learning organisation with that of the designers of a ship.

Senge (1997) believes team learning requires personal mastery through clarifying and deepening our vision and building a shared vision. However, it does not just require an aligned vision or goal, but trust and belief in effective collaboration and communication, and an ongoing commitment to developing knowledge, skills and relationships through the realisation that the goal-posts will be continually moving. Commitment to team learning requires motivation, which is helped by an aligned vision, but a coach can help with commitment through encouraging momentum and motivation.

Systems thinking is integral to team learning. It is a holistic approach to understanding and analysing complex systems that involves viewing a system as a whole and taking into account the interactions and interdependencies among its various components, rather than focusing solely on individual elements in isolation. Coaching can help teams to be aware of the reality of situations and to gain perspective when learning though systems thinking, and learn and function better though open guided discussions.

A school strategic vision may include producing happy and successful children. Everyone in the community would then align their individual or team goals with this vision. Staff have goals of producing happy and successful students, and pupils set their own goal of how to be happier or more successful through their performance in different areas of school life. Alignment occurs when all those within an organisation are aware of and working towards the strategic vision. Murray (2017) comments on members wanting purpose and how people need to define and review goals that fit the organisation's purpose.

Coaching can help to develop team learning, trust and relationships, and also alignment of the goals of individuals, or team members, with those of the school, college or university. Coaching can help to improve current performance, and also foster creativity and innovation as it helps create a safe environment where individuals trust each other and are encouraged to embrace failure as an opportunity for growth.

A coaching culture can foster continuous improvement and development through the practice of action learning.

Action learning

Senge's (1997) team learning focuses on building a learning culture within a team or organisation, while Reginald Revans' action learning is a problem-solving approach that uses collaborative learning to address real-world challenges (Pedler, 2016). They complement each other in the broader context of creating a learning-oriented and adaptive environment within teams and organisations.

Coaching promotes action and team learning by encouraging individuals and teams to reflect on their experiences, insights and challenges, leading to deeper understanding and improved decision-making. Through open dialogue and supportive feedback, coaching fosters a culture of continuous learning, empowering individuals and teams to take purposeful actions and grow collectively. Sandahl (2020) says coaching is the most sustainable approach to developing teams and that it develops a more effective and collaborative team.

Marsick and Neil (2005) describe Revan's model of action learning, in which people meet on equal terms and try to consider solutions to real-world problems, where there is no one right answer, but rather a range of possibilities.

Action learning is further described by Pedler (2016). He writes that Revans came up with two formulae for how learning is achieved: Revans' law, $L >$ or $= C$ (the rate of change) and $L = P + Q$, where L is learning, P is programmed knowledge and Q is questioning or insight. Revans believed the ability to take risks, and to question and be open to change, was key to learning:

> *In presenting action and learning as enjoined with each other, he proposes both a therapeutic process to encourage people to overcome the problems that immobilise them and as a means of invigoration and renewal through grasping the opportunities and challenge of social and organisational change.*
>
> (Pedler, 2016, p 3)

Revan's work starts with real-world problem-solving. Pedler (2016, p 13) also cites Grint (2010) and his model of three types of problems from '*critical*', requiring immediate action, to '*tame*', requiring planning, and '*wicked*', requiring real-world problem-solving, learning and distributed leadership. Good learning occurs when there is an element of challenge. Although he refers to wicked problems as those we cannot solve, I just love the term, and think we should use it for problems that are challenging but need collaboration to solve.

Examples of action learning could be pupils working in groups on a class project or staff working in teams. A coach can help create the right environment for action learning. The organisation needs to value collaboration and be willing to empower people and let them be accountable. Effective collaboration occurs where teamwork is valued and team members know how to communicate. The coach can ensure that there is an environment where people feel safe to collaborate, and potentially fail and learn from their mistakes. The coach can help staff or students by helping to add structure by allowing time for planning, goal-setting, actioning and reflecting in order for solutions to be found, and learning and improvements to occur.

The benefits of action learning can be both short and long term in nature. In the short term, as teams solve a problem together though action and reflection, they achieve a team goal. In the longer term, teams and organisations benefit further from each collaboration, as their trust and communication improve and they learn to accept challenges and learn together.

Action Learning Associates (2023) describe the impact of action learning on an organisation as developing stakeholder engagement, improved learning and performance and better change management. Further benefits include greater return on investment (ROI) and better leadership succession planning.

In a learning organisation environment that is future-focused and 'built to last', a coaching culture supports the building of relationships through the development of trust and collaboration, improved communication and improved relationships with feedback and failure through the adoption of growth mindsets. A coaching culture supports team learning and action learning, and helps individuals and organisations to transform through goal-setting and goal alignment, as well as through accepting challenge by facing 'wicked' problems. The coaching culture creates a cycle of learning and development that is fed by increased performance, motivation and happiness.

Everyone in a school can try to improve their communication and collaboration skills and develop their relationship with failure.

Benjamin Franklin famously said that if you don't have a plan to be successful, then you already have a plan for failure. Everyone in the learning organisation needs to realise that failing is an opportunity to learn, and that feedback from others, as well as learning from recognising their own strengths and weaknesses, and those of others, is important.

We all need goals, and organisations need clear goals too. These can relate to all aspects of the organisation and include profit, productivity, service and people. Organisations can then detail these goals with objectives. Teams, or individuals within an organisation, will have goals and objectives that are aligned with the organisation's goals and objectives. If organisations are looking to grow and maintain their competitive edge, they need to be learning organisations with a commitment to develop. In order to develop, an organisation needs to be aware of their current situation and see where they can improve. In order for schools to be learning organisations, coaching is the best intervention to facilitate change and improvement.

> **STAFF TRAINING DISCUSSIONS**
>
> - How do you think teachers could be encouraged to develop a growth mindset? Do you think coaching would help? Explain why/why not.
> - How beneficial would it be to have coaching as the predominant management style?
> - How might a coaching culture help to develop a happier community?
> - Would you consider that your school is a learning organisation? Do you think it should be, and if so why/why not?
> - Can you think of any situations when group coaching using the TEACHER model might be useful?

COACHING 'BOOK CLUB' SUGGESTIONS

Mindset: Changing The Way You Think to Fulfil Your Potential by Dr Carol Dweck. If you weren't sure what a growth mindset was, then this is the book to read. Dweck is a psychologist from Stanford University, and her book is full of research and case studies. If you read this book, it will hopefully raise your awareness and potentially help to improve your mindset. This book is useful for teachers, parents and even pupils if they need help developing their mindset.

The Fifth Discipline: The Art and Practice of the Learning Organization by Peter Senge. This is a really popular book aimed at business over education, but I preferred it to Senge's 2007 book on schools that learn. Senge discusses the competences required to be a successful organisation, and the book contains many interesting diagrams on models of processes.

The Happiness Advantage: The Seven Principles that Fuel Success and Performance at Work by Shawn Achor. This is a great book, and it is always uplifting to read about happiness. It is full of research and interesting examples, including the 'Let my people go surfing policy' at Patagonia, how happiness affects your peripheral vision and what the Losada line is. Supplying teachers with boxes of sweets to try to keep them happy and keep them going at the end of term helps, but this book really assists you get to the nitty gritty of happiness, and could help you consider how your school could be a happier place.

Mark. Plan. Teach by Ross Morrison McGill of @TeacherToolkit fame. This book is a great read, particularly for those new to the profession. Morrison McGill gives lots of handy tips

→

for teaching, and also lists the evidence. You can read about nudge theory and yellow box marking, and learn about the zone of proximal development. The layout is very creative, making this an interesting, informative and easy-to-read book – you can dip in and out when you have time in between marking, planning and teaching.

Chapter 4:
THE TEACHER COACHING MODEL

> **LEARNING OBJECTIVES**
>
> - To help you understand the TEACHER coaching model and provide practical advice on how to apply it.
> - To understand the importance of feedback and perspective.
> - To know how important it is to recognise achievement and have help and encouragement to form SMART goals and a plan of action.
> - To understand how time for reflection is important.

Why use the TEACHER approach?

The TEACHER model is a coaching model that has been designed specifically for use in educational organisations with teaching staff, support staff and pupils alike. It is distinguished by its approach to goal-setting and its celebration of achievements for motivation. It can be used by experienced coaches but is designed to add structure to coaching conversations for those who are new to coaching. Its strength lies in the lessons learned from the development of a long history of coaching models, the coach being allowed to convey feedback on performance and the model's design for an educational environment.

The TEACHER model is based around individuals shaping their goals after feedback, rather than starting with a goal. There are coaching models that are predominant in business and the GROW model is arguably the most widely used. It is a hugely successful model that has survived for about 40 years. It was thought to have been created in the late 1980s, and first published in 1992. Sir John Whitmore (2022) designed the GROW model for use in a sporting context, then later realised how it could be translated for use in business too. However, the model starts with a goal, and often individuals can know they want to develop but may not have a clear goal at the outset. The GROW model often works in sports as it is easy to identify goals in this setting – for example, win the match, score a goal, achieve a higher score or better time. The GROW model also translates well for many organisations, where the goals may be clear at the start. However, if using coaching in an appraisal, or with a student, while there may be a goal in mind, there may be a better goal once feedback has been discussed. It might be worth considering the child in a primary school sports match who doesn't realise you switch ends at half-time and starts heading towards the wrong goal – believe me, this happens regularly!

The model also takes feedback further and separates achievements. In 2019, Ofsted reported that 68 per cent of teachers felt the teaching profession was not valued in society. The government responded to levels of well-being in schools by recommending that schools develop staff well-being by creating a positive and collegial working environment in which staff would feel supported, valued and listened to, and where they would have an appropriate level of autonomy. MacLennan, Stead and Little (2019) wrote the HM Treasury green book guidance on wellbeing and appraisals, outlining these key considerations. Acknowledging and recognising people's efforts, achievements and contributions can make them feel valued and respected, and a coaching culture helps provide autonomy. The same applies to other staff and students, and the TEACHER coaching model can help staff and students to feel supported, valued and listened to, and help to create a more positive and collegial environment.

To make a difference to work performance and job satisfaction, social contact need not always be deep to be effective. Organisational psychologists have found that even brief encounters can form 'high quality connections' which fuel openness, energy, and authenticity among coworkers, and in turn lead to a whole host of measurable tangible gains in performance.

(Achor, 2011, p 185)

Poutanen (2018) considers social connections and describes David Rocks' SCARF model of status: certainty; autonomy; relatedness; and fairness. She writes on applying this model which considers how our brain reacts to threat and reward systems for basic survival, to our social interactions, and comments on how important being social is to humans. If we can *'understand our social brain'* we can make better connections. The main purpose of the TEACHER coaching model is for staff appraisals, in the hope that the coaching conversations are 'high quality connections', leading to greater happiness and performance.

The TEACHER model

- **T**arget and consider goals.
- **E**nlightenment and considering different perspectives and reality of situations.
- **A**chievement: recognition and celebration.
- **H**elp focus goals, and form plans of action.
- **E**ncouragement and motivation.
- **R**eflection, reviewing and improving.

The TEACHER model can be used in many areas across schools, including for lesson observation feedback and appraisals. The Organisation for Economic Co-operation and Development (OECD) comprises 38 member countries; it is dedicated to promoting policies that improve economic and social well-being worldwide. The OECD's 2013 Teaching and Learning International Survey (TALIS) indicated that 83 per cent of teachers agreed that feedback and appraisal were fair and 79 per cent felt feedback was helpful in the development of their work. These are fairly encouraging results, but they should be improved upon by using a coaching approach. The Department for Education updated its teacher appraisal and capability model policy in March 2019, following the legal framework set out in the 2013 appraisal regulations. Its model policy has an appraisal period running for 12 months. It already appears to be encouraging a coaching approach through the setting of SMART objectives.

It is worth remembering that appraisals are not the only use of the TEACHER model, which includes: staff professional development; leadership development; teacher induction; personal development for students; academic support; career guidance; behavioural support; exam preparation; conflict resolution; team-building; transition support; teacher–student relationships; special education needs support; teacher burnout prevention; technology integration; student leadership development; and motivation and engagement, to name a few.

Target

The 'Target' element is about discussing coaching and starting to consider goals. This stage involves establishing the relationship, building trust and rapport, contracting boundaries on what can be shared and with whom, exploring possible areas for growth, starting to focus on goals, and discussing what good coaching conversations and outcomes look like.

The relationship needs to be established between the coach and the coachee at the start of the cycle. This would outline when and where the coach and coachee would meet, clarify the confidentiality of the coaching agreement and explain how the coaching relationship could be ended.

Pre-meeting

During the 'Target' session of the coaching process, some pre-meeting steps need to be taken. One initial step would be to ensure the coaching conversations stand a better chance of success by considering relationships. Coaching can occur in individual or group settings and, regardless, the relationships between those involved need to be considered. If there is group coaching, then considerations would include what coaching groupings would be the most suitable, as well as matching the best coach and coachee partnerships. If lists of coaches and coaches are published, then it allows for coaches to see whether they are comfortable with the relationship. A coachee can end a relationship and if the coach's position was a paid external role, it would be equally important to create the best matches. If pupils are coaching, they may find it easier to coach in pairs, but older students could coach on their own. They may coach individuals or small groups, and these relationships would also need to be considered.

An organisation may wish to use pre-coaching surveys so they can compare them with post-coaching surveys to measure the impact of coaching within an organisation. The coaching session may be part of a staff appraisal and, if so, feedback would be collected before the session. This might involve book scrutiny and verbal feedback from interviews or peer surveys. An OECD report found teachers were more likely to find feedback useful if it was based on multiple sources of evidence.

The pre-meeting steps could be informal, with a simple chat to make arrangements for the coaching sessions, or they could easily be arranged by email. There may be a single coaching conversation, but to be more effective a series of conversations should take place. The number and duration of these meetings should be discussed, as well as the format and whether the meetings are in person or via video call. This first contact would be to sort logistics, including when and where to meet and a brief discussion of the purpose of the meetings. Pre-meeting logistics might involve some forward planning of the coaching environment.

Environment

A good environment is crucial, including *'a physical environment and relationship environment in terms of ground rules, expectations and agreements'* (Kimsey-House et al, 2011, p 17). The coach might want to consider the environment, but they may also want to bring the coachee into this decision-making process. Coaching could occur outside and even take the form of a coaching walk, but it is more likely to happen indoors. When considering the physical environment, the area to be found would be one where the coachee feels comfortable and safe. A coach may even ask a coachee to describe or draw what their ideal environment might look like. The main areas to consider would be peace and privacy, but if coaching involved children, then safeguarding would also need to be considered and use of rooms with door windows. Seating type and arrangement could also be considered in terms of comfort, eyelines and distance. Other factors to consider might include any required technology or equipment, room temperature, ventilation and lighting. McLeod (2003) discusses the principal instruments of coaching as silence, questions and challenge. For the coach and coachee to be comfortable with silence, their environment and their relationship will be important. The room colour and décor might also affect how conducive the room is to a good coaching session. A blank white room might feel a bit institutional, and a coachee might prefer a room with paintings, scatter cushions, candles and potted plants. The coach should also not forget refreshments – the coach and coachee are having a coaching conversation, which is thirsty work, so water might be advisable.

Willis (2007) comments on the impact of environments in the context of learning. This could also be applied to coaching. Interesting and stress-free environments improve focus through transmission via the reticular activating system, and filtering through the amygdala's affective filter. Willis (2007) points out that *'pleasurable associations linked with learning are more likely to release more dopamine* and that *'dopamine increases focused attention, to improve learning'*.

Pleasantries

During the first coaching conversation, trust needs to start forming between the coach and the coachee. The coach can help build this through empathy, openness, integrity, consistency, active listening and reliability. The initial conversation would be to try to put the coachee at ease, and might include pleasantries and introductions. A coach may also wish to use a conversation ladder, which is a list of questions progressing from surface-level topics to more meaningful discussions – for example, 'What is your name?', then 'Where do you live?' and moving on from there. Megginson and Clutterbuck (2005) suggest a useful getting to know you ladder. This stage is not about eliciting key personal information and values but rather about creating the right environment to put the coachee at ease.

Contracting

Once the coachee has relaxed, it is important to contract the relationship. This does not necessarily require a written contract, and can be a verbal agreement. One of the most important things to discuss is confidentiality. The coach would need to know whether anything they say will be shared with anyone else. If a coaching conversation is for an appraisal, then the information is likely to be shared with the head and the head of human resources. The coach should be allowing as much confidentiality as their role will allow, or as much as legal or ethical reasons allow. There may also be areas that the coachee would like to mention from the outset that they are not comfortable discussing or sharing. The work of psychiatrist Carl Rogers may be useful, and one idea is to visually represent in a Venn-style circle of disclosure where boundaries on different topics and with different people may lay.

If pupils are coaching, they would need to be given guidance on what they should share with other people.

Contracting does not just involve confidentiality, but can refer to how the relationship ends. This would be important to discuss in terms of setting expectations, and also in case of any breakdown in the coaching relationship or other reasons where the session ends early. Contracting might also include ground rules, including the levels of commitment, engagement and open communication required and the need for active listening, trust and respect.

After introductions, warm-up conversations and contracting have occurred, hopefully the coachee feels secure enough to start their coaching conversations. Trust is very important for a successful relationship, and this starts with self-trust by the coach and coachee.

Trust

On his website Franklin Covey (2023) describes Covey's waves of trust that build trust. The first wave is individual and self-trust, and ripples of trust flow out in waves from this. The second wave is relationship trust, which relies on consistent behaviour. The third wave is organisational trust, and the key principle underlying it is alignment. Leaders help to create structures, systems and symbols of organisational trust. The fourth wave is market or reputation, and the fifth wave is societal trust with the underlying principle of contribution. When a coach demonstrates self-trust, it means they have confidence in their coaching abilities, knowledge and ethical conduct. Coachees are more likely to trust a coach who shows self-assurance and authenticity.

Kimsey-House et al (2011) discuss trust and the role of seeking permission before giving feedback, and suggest that it is one of the key techniques for reminding the coachee that they are in charge. Relationship trust is fostered through open communication, active listening, empathy and confidentiality. Organisational trust is most easily accomplished by coaches holding accredited awards, but a demonstration that they have been trained and supported by their organisation is also effective. Market trust relates to trust in the coaching industry, which can be supported by coaches signing a code of ethics. It can also relate to trust in the school, which can be developed through establishing a coaching culture. Finally societal trust can be developed throughout the coaching relationship, as it is about serving and helping others.

Expectations

Trust will be important throughout the relationship, and open and honest conversations will help to build trust. A starting point could be a conversation about what a good coaching session might look like. Asking the coachee what they hope to have achieved at the end of the first session will help them realise that they are in control. This first stage is initiation. Although Frances Kram's (1983) work relates to mentoring, she mentions stages that apply to coaching too. Her stages of mentoring are initiation (where expectations are realised), cultivation (where meetings are most productive), satisfaction (where satisfaction is hopefully achieved by all) and redefinition (where roles are redundant and need to be redefined). The conclusion stage needs to be managed carefully, as the closure aspect is important, and both parties may feel a sense of loss or resentment as the process draws to its inevitable close. A discussion of what a good session looks like, and what will have been achieved, is part of the initiation stage.

Be kind with your time

It is probably useful at this point in the discussion to already understand how the coaching relationship will continue. This will depend on what the coaching session is for and the time allowed. Coaching could be used in a one-off session, which might be followed up by informal chats or emails, but is more likely to occur over a period of weeks. In schools, staff wear many hats: coach, cheerleader, counsellor, detective, nurse, zoo keeper – the list goes on. Pupils are also balancing being in the classroom with extra-curricular activities, catching up on homework, playing football at break, socialising and so on. A big barrier in educational institutions is finding the time to deliver coaching effectively. However, as more parties become involved in coaching, more people will see the benefits and realise how investing in coaching is worthwhile. For the coach and coachee, it will be important to know how long they have and how many meetings there will be. Flexibility may be possible, and perhaps the sessions will continue until a goal is achieved. The main point is that knowledge of the duration of the relationship will impact the aim of each individual session. Useful questions at this stage in the conversation might include asking what a good session looks like for the coachee today and how they will feel at the end. This helps remind the coachee that the coach is autonomy-supportive and helps them to realise the value of the coaching sessions. If the coach is to be 'kind with their time', they need to be aware of the impact of coaching, and how important the time spent coaching is.

Potential goals

The next step might be an initial discussion around goals. The coachee may have a clear goal in mind, may have an idea of a goal they want to shape after feedback, or may only know that they want to develop and improve, but have no clear idea of a goal. If the goal is already decided by someone other than the coachee as part of a capability process for staff, then the conversation cannot really follow coaching processes, due to the ownership of the goal. In this case, mentoring may be more appropriate.

Purpose

If the coach and coachee know how long their relationship is to last, they will know how long they can spend on the Target stage, including exploration of goals. Goal-setting gives us purpose in life, and if a goal has not come to surface then discussions about purpose may help. A coachee may feel more comfortable with just a discussion of purpose, but activities can also be used. A coach might find it easier to structure a coaching session by using a set of coaching cards to guide them through the order of the conversation and activities. One diagram, or coaching card activity, that could be discussed or drawn as an activity is an *ikigai* model. *Ikigai* is a Japanese term meaning 'reason for living', The concept of *ikigai* has been represented in a model that looks like a Venn diagram with four overlapping circles with *ikigai* at their heart. The four circles represent what you love, what you are good at, what the world needs and what you can be paid for. An ice-breaking activity or discussion on *ikigai* could help uncover the skills and values of the coachee and also generate a discussion on goals. The coaching conversation might continue with a discussion on what the coachee thinks their goals are.

To continue a conversation on purpose, it could be useful to discuss different categories of goals. A conversation starter could be looking at a wheel of life, a circular chart that is easily created using an Excel pie radar chart. The chart has different areas of a person's life dotted around the circumference of career/school/work, money, health, friends, family, personal growth, spiritual, and fun and recreation. The coachee is encouraged to rank each area out of ten and to discuss the bumpy ride.

This activity is designed to raise awareness of areas that might need developing, and is useful for initial talks. Another way to consider purpose is through categorising goals as learning and development goals, attitude and behaviour goals, and performance and standard goals. Learning and development goals focus on acquiring new knowledge and skills; attitude and behaviour goals aim to change mindsets and behaviours; and performance and standards goals concentrate on achieving specific outcomes and meeting performance benchmarks. For teachers, this would mean the teaching standards. All three types of goals are essential in personal and professional development, and they often intersect and complement each other to drive overall growth and success. Discussing these types of goals might help the coachee gain further clarity on their purpose, and what their goal might be.

If the coachee is still unclear about which areas they should be aiming at for goal-setting, then using the three good things exercise might help. This activity is designed to take place over a number of days where the individual is asked to write down three good things every day. Although the exercise is designed to increase feelings of gratitude and well-being, the exercise could also be useful for spotting patterns. This is made even easier using Microsoft Forms. If the coachee completes a simple daily three-question survey, the insights report in the results could show any word patterns. Looking at these patterns might help identify skills and values, strengths and weaknesses, and help with goal formulation.

However, a goal may still not have been formed at this stage. For a staff member, a discussion on the organisation's goals may help. If the coachee discusses the whole-school vision and organisational goals, they may be able to see where they fit into the plan, and consider their purpose and own goal. However, the coachee —whether they are a staff member or student — may need enlightenment on their strengths and weaknesses before setting a goal.

For the maths teachers reading this, in simple terms:

$$\text{Target} = \text{Pre-meeting} + \text{Pleasantries} + \text{Contracting} + \text{Expectations} + \text{Time management} + \text{Purpose}$$

Enlightenment

'Enlightenment' is about considering feedback, different perspectives and the reality of situations. This is the stage at which motivations will be discussed, and feedback will be shared on actions, skills, knowledge, attitudes, behaviours and emotions. Strengths and weaknesses of the coachee will be explored and barriers will be considered.

Hill (2019) comments that feedback should be timely, non-judgemental, clearly communicated and future focused. She says feedback should be checked for bias, and there should be sufficient delving into situations before conclusions are formed. This supports a model of goal-setting after feedback.

Stephen Covey (2004) uses the analogy of sharpening the saw. He tells the story of a woodcutter sawing wood and actually performing better because he rests every now and then. Sawing dulls the blade, so resting could provide time to sharpen the blade. The moral is that in order to perform well, it is important to take time for self-renewal, and this can take the form of physical, social/emotional, mental or spiritual self-renewal. I like to consider this same story in terms of feedback, and also considering Einstein's ideas on insanity and the idea that insanity is doing the same thing over and over, while expecting different results. The woodcutter needed feedback: he needed to either self-assess or be told by someone else that his saw was dull and it was time to sharpen the saw in order to generate improved performance.

The Enlightenment stage of the TEACHER coaching conversation can be based on a four-stage reflective growth model. The stages are self-assessment, feedback, perspective and clarity.

Self-assessment

The first stage of Enlightenment is self-assessment. This is where the coachee is asked to comment on their own strengths and weaknesses, any barriers they see to their development, and their feelings about where they are and where they want to be. This emotional aspect is for acknowledging and addressing the coachee's emotional responses to various situations, challenges or opportunities.

Favell's (2016) ASK ABE model could be used to guide this part of the conversation. This is where reflections are what you see when you look at in the mirror, and how people should be encouraged to look at themselves in terms of their actions, skills, approaches, behaviours and emotional control.

Feedback

The next step in Enlightenment is feedback. There is a conscious competence feedback model, which is sometimes represented on a spectrum from conscious competence (what you know you are good at) to conscious incompetence (what you know you are not good at yet) to unconscious incompetence (where you didn't know you could not do it) to unconscious competence (where you can do something so well that you can do it without thinking about it). Feedback from others can help raise awareness on an individual's unconscious competence and incompetence but also help motivate them by raising their awareness of what they do well, whether they know it or not.

Coaching is about conversations and asking questions, and coaching is not a telling approach. This needs to be considered when discussing feedback. The coach may have gathered feedback on the individual, but should try not to just pass this information on, particularly with any accompanying judgements, but rather try to guide the coachee to discover the feedback through questioning techniques. This doesn't always work – it certainly doesn't work with my husband when I ask him to think about clothing choices, and whether he thinks he has made a good choice or not, by wearing a ripped top inside out. However, when I have an agenda, I am trying to persuade and judge, and this is not coaching. If it is not possible to guide the coachee to discover the feedback, then permission should be asked to give feedback.

Feedforward

On its teaching and learning hub website, the University of Bath discusses assessment for learning and the difference between feedback and feedforward: *'Feedback focuses on a student's current performance while feedforward looks ahead to how students can improve both current and subsequent assessments.'* The feedforward approach would be more useful in a coaching conversation. There is also research on issues with feedback, which include students not understanding feedback and how to action it, feedback being more individualised, lack of engagement with feedback, time constraints on giving effective feedback, feedback's association with comments on summative assessment and with justifying a summative mark rather than improving learning, and feedback being untimely and not specific.

If coaching is used for an appraisal following a lesson observation, it would be important to have the conversation in a timely manner following the observation. It is important for the coach to remember that coaching is not about giving feedback but rather asking questions so the coachee can discover the feedback for themselves.

RISE feedback

There are many different models of feedback. FAST feedback stands for frequent, accurate, specific and timely. The SBI model stands for situation, behaviour and impact, where the behaviour is considered rather than assuming what the other person is thinking. CEDAR stands for content, examples, diagnosis, actions and review. The BEER model is behaviour, effect, expectation and result. The AID model can also be useful; it stands for action, impact and do. AID is useful for behaviour and may work best when delivering feedback on soft skills. AID is explaining to the person what they did that could be improved upon and questioning the impact it had, and the 'do' discussion relates to what could be done better. The coach could remind the coachee of a particular situation or action and, using feedforward, guide the coachee to consider its impact and what they might do in the future. The Pendleton Feedback model is also commonly used:

> *Clarify any points of information, state the facts. The learner then identifies what they think went well. The teacher adds their observations and thoughts and reinforces the positive points. The learner then adds what went less well and what they would do differently next time. The teacher then adds their thoughts and recommendations for next time.*
>
> (Worton and Ippolito, 2014, p 8)

RISE Feedback is another model that can be used in the Enlightenment stage.

Respectful feedback

RISE stands for Respectful, Informative, Specific, and Evidence-based. It provides a framework for delivering constructive feedback that is effective, supportive and focused on growth and improvement. When providing feedback, it is essential to be empathetic and respectful of the recipient. This means avoiding using judgemental or negative language and approaching the conversation with empathy and kindness. Respectful feedback is also timely, as it considers the fact that the receiver may be anxious while waiting for the feedback.

Framing and feedback sandwiches

If the coach cannot guide the coachee to discover the feedback, and it has to be delivered, or told, it is important to deliver respectful feedback. A range of questioning techniques can be used. Karen Pery of Pery Coaching and Consulting uses the term 'framing'. She identifies that people find it hard to hear criticism and frames negative aspect with phrases that prepare the coachee. This could be done by seeking permission: 'Is it okay if I give you some feedback that might be hard to hear?' Another technique could be a feedback sandwich, where the negative aspects are sandwiched between two positive aspects.

Informative feedback

Constructive feedback should also be relevant and informative, and provide valuable insights to the recipient regarding their performance, behaviour or actions. I once requested feedback after an interview and my main takeaway was that I was told I had dressed well. I did not consider this particularly informative as it did not deliver an insight that helped me develop. Just as when teachers are marking, they would probably not highlight every spelling mistake of a dyslexic, it is important to focus on the most relevant and informative aspects. The skill of the coach in helping manage the conversation can be important, as they will be beginning to understand the goals of the coachee and will have awareness of how long can be dedicated to feedback in the coaching relationship. Feedback is from an external source and might include interviews, book evidence, achievements, engagement in training, observations and so on. Feedback is better if it comes from multiple sources, but it is important to be aware there may be bias. The coach can try to focus the conversation on the feedback that is informative and most likely to help the coachee develop.

Specific feedback

The next stage in RISE when it comes to delivering feedback for growth is specificity. This is crucial in feedback and entails being clear and precise about the behaviours or actions that need addressing. Specific feedback not only details what has been identified but why that might be important. If the coach has given feedback, they could ask the coachee to try to think about why it was important This links with the last stage, where feedback becomes more credible and effective when it is backed by evidence or examples. Feedback should be supported by objective data, observations or specific incidents that highlight the areas needing improvement.

Evidence

The final element is evidence. This means examples of specific incidents, as well as examples or data that demonstrate the coachee's performance or behaviour, are shared. During this stage, you would also need to consider confidentiality or the effect of sharing where the feedback has come from. If people think their feedback is anonymous, they may offer different feedback than if they are able to be identified. It is important to consider how the identity might be given away through the situation or the context of the feedback. This would also need to be considered in a whole-school approach. If one person shared the name of a person who gave feedback, this might lead to an expectation, and whereas this might be a positive experience for one coachee, that might not be the case for another.

By following the RISE feedback model, you can create a supportive and constructive feedback environment.

Johari window

The Johari window is an excellent feedback model that could be used to guide this part of the conversation. American psychologists Joseph Luft and Harrington Ingham developed the Johari (a combination of their names) window model in 1955. The model has four quadrants, which indicate what is known by the person about themselves and what is known by others about them. The four windows describe the open area, which is what the person and others know about them; the hidden area, which is what the person knows about themselves but does not share freely; the blind area, which is known by others but not by the individual; and the exciting unknown area, which is something not yet discovered about the individual by them or others. Not everybody has the same-size quadrants so if this is used as a coaching activity, the coachee might need to consider this when they draw their two-by-two grid, as the quadrants would not be squares. This model might be useful for discussing different perspectives.

Perspective

The third area within the Enlightenment level of the TEACHER model is perspective. We can sometimes only see things from one point of view, and widening our perspective can be important. There is a famous basketball experiment that psychologists conducted where people were asked to count the number of passes made by a particular team. Afterwards, they were asked what they thought about the giant gorilla. Forty-six per cent of the observers missed the giant gorilla, as they were so focused on one element of the game (Achor, 2011). It can be useful to widen our perspective further than just looking at things from one other point of view, and to consider multiple perspectives.

Edward de Bono (1985) describes perspective in his book *Six Thinking Hats.* He describes a story where people disagree about the description of a house viewed by each of them from different angles. This is similar to the parable about the blind men finding an elephant, and each thinking they have found different things from snakes (its trunk) to tree trunks (its legs). De Bono encourages parallel thinking to gain a clearer perspective, with team members collaborating on thinking processes so they have a more complete picture and can make more informed decisions. De Bono describes wearing different hats of different colours: the white hat represents considering facts and figures, the black represents caution and looking for problems, green is for creative ideas, red is an emotional view, blue is for organisation and drawing things together, and yellow is for positive and optimistic thinking. The thinking hats are often used in teams when considering a problem, but a coach could try to encourage a coachee to look at different problems by considering what they would look like from the perspective of wearing each coloured hat. Matthew Syed (2019) believes cognitive diversity is key to humanity's progress. The coach can encourage cognitive diversity in the coachee and therefore encourage the consideration of different perspectives.

Various other activities can be used to gain perspective. McLeod (2003) talks about conscious perception and asking the coachee to really consider situations through asking questions such as 'Who says?', 'How do you know?', 'Always?' and 'Can you think of an exception?'

A further activity could be applying the Pareto principle to try to gain perspective on performance. Vilfredo Pareto devised the Pareto Principle, which states that 20 per cent of your activities account for 80 per cent of your results (Koch, 2004). The coachee could be asked to identify the 20 per cent by writing down their most productive tasks and then considering how this might help them move forward.

Role-play

Role-play can also help provide perspective. A coachee could be asked to play different roles in situations concerning them. They might consider an interaction and assume the role of the other person to help them gain perspective. Another role-play includes the use of time and asking coachees what they would say if they went back and spoke to a younger version of themselves, or if a future version visited them. There are some great apps for ageing a photo of someone to really bring this activity to life. Finally, another role-play involves taking a helicopter view, or a broad and high-level perspective on a situation. It is similar to the concept of a helicopter hovering above and looking down at a landscape to see the big picture and understand the context rather than being immersed in the details on the ground. It allows the coachee to see patterns, connections and potential consequences that may not be evident when they are focused on the minutiae.

Clarity

The final stage is clarity. This is the stage where the coachee is guided to consider all the feedback and the perspectives offered, and endeavours to gain clarity on their situation to help them with goal selection. The PEG model may be helpful to guide this element of the conversation; it stands for Performance, Expectation and Gap. The coachee will hopefully have improved their perspective and knowledge of their performance or their own strengths and weaknesses; they can then look at expectations – what others expect of them – and self-expectations, and try to consider how they can close the gap between performance and expectations. Identifying this gap will help them to decide a goal or goals.

Another activity involves considering the desired state. The coach could try to encourage the coachee to assess their current situation and then think about their desired state – how where they are now makes them feel, and how they hope to feel in the future. The coach helps the coachee envision a future state that aligns with their goals, values and aspirations, allowing them to explore the emotions, motivations and potential obstacles associated with achieving that desired state. By bridging the gap between the current situation and the desired state, the coachee gains clarity and motivation, making it easier to set actionable steps towards their goals.

Self-assessment, feedback and perspective help to achieve clarity. Some coachees may find different stages harder to explore than others. Meister, Willyerd and Zemke (2010) write about differences and how those in Generation Y are seeking a purpose for their work rather than a balance in their work, which leads to a thirst for feedback. They discuss micro-feedback and, through familiarity with social media, creating online feedback with limited characters. It is important to use the best tools and the best questions for each individual.

The development of a coaching culture will help everyone with their relationship with feedback as it builds a growth mindset. A culture where coaching will be embedded will see all parties become better at accepting, requesting and giving feedback. Accepting feedback involves listening to it actively, adding perspective to the feedback by being aware of the filters of others, thanking the person for being generous in giving feedback, then evaluating the feedback and acting on it:

$$\text{Enlightenment} = \text{Self-Assessment} + \text{RISE Feedback} + \text{Perspective} + \text{Clarity}$$

Achievement

This stage of the model focuses on recognition and celebration of achievements. It is about ensuring achievements are noticed, recorded and celebrated.

The enlightenment stage is about looking at strengths and weaknesses, so it could be argued that achievements have already been discussed. However, the achievement element ensures there is a key focus on the coachee's achievements and, in addition to noticing the achievements, is about recording them and understanding how celebrating them may help to achieve more.

The OECD (2012) *Teaching in Focus* report summarises that

> *effective appraisal and feedback systems can impact what happens in the classroom but many teachers feel they are not getting appropriate recognition or feedback on their work. A good way to improve teachers' self-efficacy and student learning is to value teachers' innovative work and to publicly recognise teachers' work.*

If coaching is part of an appraisal, this can be an opportunity to note and celebrate achievements formally. If coaching is for self-development, then it would involve making a note of achievements on a personal development plan, and if coaching is for 'tutoring' a pupil, it would include helping pupils to record their achievements.

The Chartered Management Institute (2018) states that research shows organisations that invest in coaching for management and leadership development programmes see on average a 23 per cent increase in organisational performance and a 32 per cent increase in people performance. They note how coaching can increase motivation, as staff feel valued and staff turnover is reduced. If coaching is eliciting such a return on performance, it is important to note, discuss and celebrate the performance achievements of the coachee.

Further support on the benefits of celebrating achievement comes from the work of humorous public speaker and author of *The Happiness Advantage* Shawn Achor (2011). He speaks about how, through repeating actions and practising changing how you think, it is possible to filter what you think, and rewire your brain. You can practise looking for more positive aspects of your life and celebrating achievements. As a Harvard professor, he commented on the study of Tetris users and, much like the coloured blobs, or retinal after-images you see after staring at lights, he noted how studies showed that Tetris use affected the brain, and used the example as how after-images may make people want to jigsaw together boxes on shelves like Tetris shapes in an OCD fashion when they are at the supermarket. He comments on cognitive after-images and how, because of this effect, repetition of an activity – for example, celebrating small successes – can reframe our thinking, making us happier and more productive.

Amabile and Kramer (2011) also support celebrating achievements. They comment on the importance of appreciating small wins, and advocate noting and sharing your success. They also maintain that it is important not to be afraid to reward yourself. I demonstrate this magnificently in report writing season: one completed report = one Galaxy Minstrel! Your body responds when you accomplish something: dopamine is released and the reward centre of your brain is activated – you feel a sense of pride.

Noticing achievement types and strengths

During the Achievement stage of the conversation, it may help to consider what achievements are. Some people may find their achievements harder to recognise than others. It is important to consider the impact of perspective and to consider all achievements. The coachee may not consider something they have achieved as noteworthy, while others may believe it is. Conversely, there may be something that the coachee has achieved that is of particular significance or importance to them, but others may not hold the achievement in such high regard. All achievements should be considered, but discussing the perspective might be useful.

There are various ways of considering achievements: short versus long term, individual versus team, academic versus non-academic, tangible versus intangible, social versus individual impact, skills based versus outcome based, milestones versus process achievements and personal versus professional achievements. If a coachee is struggling to note their achievements, it may help for the coach to work through these areas, with examples, and ask the coachee to think about their own achievements in each area.

Using 'At My Best' cards could be another activity to nurture discussions on achievements. These are beautiful cards from atmybest.com, with adjectives describing strengths. The coachee chooses the cards that best represent them. This may help to focus their thoughts on why they think these are their strengths and what they have achieved to support each strength.

Recording

Staff and pupils need to consider how they are recording their achievements. Online platforms can be used, or OneNote, or even just a notebook. Certificates could even be framed. As wife to a former soldier, we used to own a standard decorated downstairs toilet – by this I mean it had magnolia woodchip wallpaper and had a wall full of photographs of soldiers and my husband's achievements (he is modest – I was probably more instrumental in this). If you know any soldiers, you may well be aware of what I am talking about. Maybe teachers should have standard teachers' toilets and frame their first aid, fire-safety and growth-mindset course attendance certificates. Teachers' achievements could be added to email signatures, celebrated on staff noticeboards, in newsletters, in emails, in notelets or letters, at staff meetings or even in assemblies, alongside pupil celebrations of success. These achievements need to be noted for a curriculum vitae, a record of achievement or a personal or professional development plan.

Celebrating

Once achievements have been noted and the way they will be recorded has been considered, the coach can help the coachee to celebrate their achievement. The coach may help by praising the achievement, but they should also help the coachee become aware of what they have achieved and encourage them to celebrate their own success. Even celebrating small wins or marginal gains is important, as it helps drive further motivation. Acknowledging and celebrating achievements fosters a positive mindset and reinforces intrinsic motivation, leading to improved overall performance and greater happiness:

Achievements = Noticing + Recording + Celebrating

Choice

The Choice stage is about continuing to explore a choice of goal and options for achieving goals. This is the stage where the coach probably needs to apply most of their skills. The coach will be structuring the conversation, and managing the time of the conversations, but should not accelerate the conversation by offering answers. As much as this part is about the coachee having choice, it is also about the coachee and their requirement to firm up some decisions. The coach needs to be mindful that they remain non-directive, but they also need to try to facilitate decisions.

Goal or goals

Closer focus on a goal is one area within the Choice stage. The coachee should now have a goal in mind, or may even have several goals that they need to prioritise. The coach can help the coachee with goal selection, goal prioritisation and options for plans for achieving the goal. The coach can help the coachee by mirroring back to them what they have heard the coachee say regarding their targets for growth. By starting a question with 'I heard you say that', the coach is demonstrating their listening skills and is helping the coachee to decide on their goal. Scaling techniques might be useful to decide between goals – for example, on a scale of 1 to 10, how much impact will each goal have? Pegg (1999) has many useful questions that can be used – for example, 'What would you like to happen instead?'

Options

The next choices are about generating options for moving forward. 'Creative brainstorming', as in the ACHIEVE model, could be encouraged by exploring various possibilities and strategies to reach goals. Questions such as 'What are your options for moving forward' are used. Thinking outside the box can be useful when it comes to options, and activities may help to generate ideas. There is a useful set of cards called Pip Decks on the site pipdecks.com, which offers a range of activities for brainstorming and idea generation. The coach can help the coachee to consider their emotions around different options

The choice for moving forward should be discussed, but other options should be considered before the first option is seized immediately. Once one option for development has been discussed, the coach can ask 'What else?'. The coach can help the coachee consider alternatives and critically assess the pros and cons of each option. McLeod (2003) suggests numerous useful coaching activities, including asking the coachee to try to contradict themselves to gain perspective. The coach can help the coachee to consider the feasibility, risks, resources required and alignment with the coachee's values and long-term vision.

Further clarification can be achieved through the use of Cartesian questions. These were created by René Descartes and open the mind to options and possibilities.

The four Cartesian questions are:

1. What would happen if you did …?
2. What would happen if you didn't do …?
3. What wouldn't happen if you did …?
4. What wouldn't happen if you didn't do …?

Barriers or obstacles

Conversation on barriers can also be facilitated, and barriers or obstacles identified, with discussion about how they can be overcome. Root cause analysis (RCA) addresses the deeper issue of a problem. The coach can help the coachee to define the barrier and look at the who, what, how, when, where and why of the problem. The coach can ask the coachee which options, as solutions, are the most attractive, and what they would choose to do if barriers such as time and money were overcome. They can also help them look at barriers by considering Covey's (2004) sphere of influence. This is a model of a circle of influence within a circle of concern. It can be used to help consider actionable options for achieving their goals by focusing on what they can control within their circle of influence.

Another activity could be using the 5 Whys technique (Serrat, 2017). This method was created by Japanese inventor Sakichi Toyoda, who founded Toyota Industries. He suggested that you should define a problem, or an obstacle that is holding you back, and try and think of five reasons why it is happening. Many more activities, which could be used in a coaching conversation (although they are listed as 75 ideas for mentoring), are listed by Phillips-Jones (2003).

There can be simple steps taken to overcome barriers and the coach can increase the coachee's awareness of how obstacles can be overcome. Achor (2011) describes a '20 second rule' and the fact that humans often take the path of least resistance over a desired behaviour; making the better choice can be as simple as making it within 20 seconds. He comments on runners who find that the 'easiest' option is to go for a run rather than take their trainers off when they have dressed to this stage. Consider Toyoda's 'why not' discussions and whether the coachee needs to consider whether they are just looking at the path of least resistance.

Priorities

The coachee may continue with more than one goal, but can be coached to focus on one or a few, and prioritise their goals. Encouraging the coachee to make a simple list to aid prioritising might help. A simple activity might be to think of the goals in a hot-air balloon that is sinking, and to 'throw out' and refine the list of goals that are left.

The next choice is to make a decision on what the goal is and what steps need to be taken. The coach can facilitate the coachee's decision-making process by helping them to clarify their values and priorities, and to understand the potential consequences of their choices. Discussing motivations might help. The Schwartz theory of basic values is a circular model of values and the motivations each expresses, and could be useful to consider (Schwartz, 2012).

The coach would need to structure the conversation and consider how long should be spent on deliberating options. A study at Stanford University looked at brain activity and indecisiveness, and found that when people spent too long deliberating, they were less inclined to consider new evidence. Although you wouldn't want to decide on options with the flip of a coin, the think-blink technique might help to test intuition by making a decision while a coin is flipped and before it lands.

Rob Lowe is quoted as saying that any time an opportunity scares you enough, you should seriously consider saying yes. If fear is an issue, there is a useful technique described by McLeod (2003), which is about achieving an anchored state. This is where you consider a relaxed time and associate it with a trigger for calmness, such as touching two fingers together. The coach can also help the coachee to consider whether they are not considering a particular goal or particular options due to fear. In what he terms the 'hedgehog principle', Collins (2001) describes how hedgehogs are very good at rolling into balls to protect themselves. He uses this as an analogy for knowing what you are good at. He also describes 'Big Hairy Audacious Goals' (BHAGs);

the coach might like to try and discuss BHAGS (bee-hags) with the coachee and whether their choice of goal and options to achieve it are 'big, hairy and audacious' or whether they have smaller goals and simpler options in mind.

The choice stage is a dynamic and interactive process that requires active engagement and collaboration between the coach and coachee. By carefully considering each of these components, the coaching relationship can be strengthened, and the coachee can effectively progress towards achieving their desired outcomes.

Choice = Goal or Goals + Options + Priorities

Help

The Help stage is where the coachee is helped to make their goals SMART (specific, measurable, achievable, relevant and time-bound) and is assisted to plan the achievement of the goals, which allows for progress to be monitored and marginal gains and milestones to be recognised.

Locke and Latham's (1990) goal-setting theory has five principles: clarity, challenge, commitment, feedback and complexity. Clarity is about ensuring that the goal is specific and clear; the goal should be challenging enough to be motivating to ensure commitment – consider Grint's (2010) 'wicked' challenges and Collins' (2001) 'BHAG's. Locke's research found that in 90 per cent of cases, having specific and challenging goals in place led to higher performance than setting goals that could be reached easily. Commitment is also helped by setting SMART goals, and goals that are set by the individual create autonomy and further commitment. Feedback and progress on goals are also important, as is the complexity – which can be helped by the use of planning steps, or marginal gains towards the final goal.

SMART and ADDIE

The ADDIE model was created by Florida State University for the military in the 1970s. ADDIE stands for Analysis, Design, Development, Implementation and Evaluation, and was developed as a guideline to create effective training materials. The ADDIE model can be useful to consider when creating a plan to achieve the goal and for writing it down.

The first stage of the plan using the ADDIE model is to make the goal SMART. The coach can ask the coachee whether their goal is SMART by explaining the different elements and asking the coachee to check and amend their goal as required. The goal needs to be specific. The coach can use the examples of Aladdin and his genie, or of Midas and his golden touch, to make sure the coachee understands the importance of being specific when goal-setting. The goal also needs to be measurable – that is, the coachee needs to know whether they have achieved it. The goal should not be unachievable, and the coachee also needs to ensure their goal is relevant and aligned with their own values and organisational values. Finally, the goal needs to have a target date for achievement.

Plan

Design and Develop are the next stages. All coaching relationships are different and it is important for the coach to consider how the coachee will want their action plan designed and how they will want to monitor their progress. An individual may prefer the logical layout of a timeline, a table in Word or a creative diagram, or may prefer something more visual to highlight their plan and its progress. Microsoft Planner is a useful tool, as is using Excel as a Gantt chart. Microsoft also has apps for tracking goals, such as Viva, which can be used within Teams. The ADDIE model was created for developing training programmes, and if using ADDIE for a development plan, it is easier to consider these two levels together as in how the plan will be designed and developed by putting more meat on its bones.

One way of putting more detail into a development plan is by considering time and resources. A further action is to consider the goal or goals and think about the objectives and milestones that can be recorded to check progress along the way. Looking at the shorter term objectives required to achieve a bigger goal can be motivating, as otherwise the change may seem too big and unobtainable. Senge (1997) uses the analogy of boiling a frog, an experiment I hope he has not tested. Apparently, a frog will hop out if placed in a pan of boiling water, but will lie back and relish the delight of its bath if the water temperature slowly increases because it will not notice the incremental changes in temperature.

Marginal gains

Monitoring marginal gains or small wins, or even just monitoring to check progress, is important in a plan. Desmond Tutu once said that there is only one way to eat an elephant, which is one bite at a time. This principle is the same as that applied by Dave Brailsford, the British Cycling performance director, who made a huge impact on British cycling success. His story is explained in the brilliant book *Atomic Habits* by James Clear (2018). He explains how 'marginal gains', even those giving just 1 per cent improvement, accrue and have an impact. Brailsford had the inside of the mechanical trucks painted white so dust would show up. This small change was not going to win anyone an Olympic cycling medal, but it added to other small changes he made in every area, from better pillows for a better night's sleep, to better cycling suits and massage gels: these incremental changes had an overall impact. The coachee should have a plan where they have considered marginal gains and smaller objectives that will help them succeed.

Kaizen

Kaizen is a Japanese term meaning continuous improvement. It can be traced back to post-war efforts to rebuild the Japanese economy and is linked with the Toyota car industry. It is a concept that emphasises making small, incremental changes and improvements over time to achieve significant progress. Applying *kaizen* to goal-setting and plans involves incorporating continuous improvement practices into the pursuit of objectives. This means reviewing the plan and continually thinking about small ways to take steps to move closer to the end goal. When applying the principle of *kaizen*, it is worth considering Clear's (2018) thoughts on habit stacking and the impact of changing the environment. He says that *'your habits change depending on the room you are in, and the cues in front of you. Environment is the invisible hand that shapes human behaviour'* and also that *'people who make a specific plan for when and where they will perform a new habit, are more likely to follow through* (Clear, 2018, p 82).

Implementing the plan

Implement and Evaluate are the next stages of ADDIE and this applies to implementing, or following the plan, and evaluating the plan and recording progress, and also evaluation and reflection once the goal is achieved, so the lessons learned can be applied when a future goal is set.

In *The Fred Factor*, Mark Sanborn (2005) talks about implementation. He also discusses thoughtfulness, kindness and how some people make it their mission to be extraordinary, not just ordinary. He uses the example of his postman, Fred, who is extraordinary because he values what he does and tries to do his job well, offering excellent service to others. Sanborn thinks we should try to have more of an impact by discovering other 'Freds'. He uses the acronym FRED: Find, Reward, Educate,

Demonstrate. Sanborn believes that valuing what you do is important if you are to be extraordinary, and says that you don't bring much value to what you do when you don't see much meaning in it. Sanborn thinks people will only know how to be ordinary if they are taught only ordinary subjects and skills, and organisations should be teaching employees to be extraordinary. He describes four principles related to the Fred factor and being extraordinary: everyone makes a difference; success is built on relationships; you should continually create value for others; and you can reinvent yourself regularly.

Sanborn (2005) also describes implementation and the difference between activity and accomplishment. He discusses the abundance of ideas of how to be a good 'Fred' as IQ, which he defines as being an implementation quotient, and talks about how some people may have good ideas but don't act on them. To be a good 'Fred', you need to have ideas about how to work better or be kind, helpful, thoughtful and so on – but you also need to implement them:

> Help = SMART Goal + Plan + Implementation.

Encouragement

The Encouragement stage is about encouragement and motivation, and ensuring the coachee remains motivated and supported as they move closer to achieving their goal. This stage is about discussion of motivation during the goal-setting stage and motivation to action the goal. This stage involves the coach providing encouragement and support, and the coachee recognising the importance of self-motivation.

Extrinsic motivation

Cook and Artino (2016) describe five different contemporary models of motivation: expectancy-value, attribution, social cognitive, goal orientation and self- determination. Studer et al (2016) discuss different expectancy-value models, including that of Victor Vroom from 1964 where motivation is determined by two factors: expectancy, or probability that a wanted or 'instrumental' outcome is achieved through the behaviour or action, and how much the individual values the desired outcome; and that 'motivation = expectancy × value'. They furthered the research by looking at the effect of 'illusory control', where individuals thought they had more control over a situation than they actually did, and found that manipulating illusory control increased motivation. The extrinsic and intrinsic nature of motivation is also important. Extrinsic motivation refers to the type of motivation that comes from external factors or rewards, such as money, recognition, praise, grades or other tangible or external benefits, rather than from within oneself. The coach can help provide social benefits through offering praise and other encouragement. The coach can also help the coachee to consider their intrinsic motivation.

Visualisation

Expectancy-value models and intrinsic motivation intersect in terms of how expectations of success and perceived value can impact a person's intrinsic motivation to engage in a behaviour. Motivation is often driven by expectations of success. If the coach is using an expectancy-value model, they might use visualisation techniques. Visualisation is about getting the coachee to think about their goals and see, smell, hear and feel what achieving that goal will be like. Ritt (2002) discusses goals and the power of visual images. He comments how early humans, with less established oral communication, were likely to have had a vivid mind's eye and a skill for visual images. He also discusses the importance of visualising what you would look like when you have achieved a level of success and using this to motivate you. You can visualise a happier or more successful version of yourself, and let yourself feel what that version of you would be like.

Australian psychologist Alan Richardson (1967) tested the power of visualisation in basketball. He had three groups. One group of players practised shooting hoops every day for 20 days; one group only practised on the first and last days; and one group did the same but spent 20 minutes every day visualising successful basketball shots. The last group proved to be almost as successful as the group that practised every day. Visualisation could help the coachee, and help them visualise the process and the outcome.

A visualisation activity could be on the process or the outcome and could be helped by discussing or creating a visual. The coachee may wish to make a photo collage of their goals and may choose to use it as a screensaver. Building on visualisation, Gail Matthews, a psychology professor at Dominican University in California, did a study on goal setting with 267 participants (Dominican University, 2015). She found that you are 33 per cent more likely to achieve your goals just by writing them down. Further studies increased this figure to 42 per cent. It is important to write your goals down. I had a goal of writing a book.

The second motivation model is on attribution. This is where the coachee may be motivated by considering what they think earlier success is attributed to. The coach could ask the coachee to think about what caused earlier successes and ask the coachee to use this knowledge to keep them motivated to achieve their current goal.

Social cognitive is the third type, and includes ideas including those from Bandura. This relates to self-efficacy and interactions between personal, behavioural and environmental factors. Motivation is affected by the way individuals feel about themselves, and how they are motivated to repeat the behaviours based on the social responses and consequences they receive when they imitate a behaviour. The coach can try to find out how much the coachee will want to rely on them for the social response of encouragement.

A further motivational model is goal orientation. This can be mastery, or a performance approach, or even performance avoidance. The coach can help the coachee to find out whether they are motivated by mastering content, doing better than others or the rather negative glass half-empty drive to just perform less poorly than others. This discussion could be driven through discussing famous motivational quotes. Rees (2017) has a great selection from Aristotle to Sylvester Stallone.

Intrinsic motivation and SDT

The final model is based on self-determination theory (SDT), and is related to intrinsic motivation that leads people to act purely to satisfy their curiosity or desire for mastery. Cook and Artino (2016) describe this as where intrinsic and internalised motivations are promoted by feelings of competence, autonomy and relatedness. Deci and Ryan's SDT model says that the first assumption of self-determination theory is *'that a need for growth as a human being drives behaviour. People are always actively seeking to grow and improve'* (Lopez-Garrido, 2023).

Maslow's hierarchy of needs

A useful tool for considering motivation can be to draw a pyramid, or create one on Excel, to represent Maslow's (1943) hierarchy model. The factors that affect motivation can depend on where they are on Maslow's model. This is where people are in stages within a pyramid that is built on the foundations of physical and survival needs, to safety and security, to love and belonging, esteem and finally self-actualisation. Developments of the model have considered how we might climb the pyramid and then slip down before climbing again. This might reflect our environment or different stages in our life.

The bottom level of the pyramid is physiological needs, or sometimes physiological and biological needs. These are our basic requirements for operating, or for surviving, and include, air, water, shelter and food. The model is often redefined to suit different situations.

The second stage is safety and our needs for safety, security, shelter and stability. This level includes security of body, employment, resources, family, health and property. Moving up, we reach the belonging level, where our needs are social and are about being accepted and included. Needs are centred around a need for belonging and being loved, whether it is friends, family, intimacy or community.

The esteem level is concerned with self-esteem, confidence, achievement, accomplishment, status and respect. If we consider this in the education context, it could be whether a school gets good academic results, wins scholarships or has successful sports teams and talented orchestras.

The pinnacle is self-actualisation. Some models include this with transcendence, fulfilling potential, self-mastery, morality, creativity, problem-solving, spontaneity, acceptance and lack of prejudice. Kishima and Koga (2017) discuss purpose in their book *The Courage to Be Disliked*. Aetiology is the study of the cause, and teleology is the study of the purpose of a given phenomenon, according to Kishimi and Koga. We can focus on our purpose and our goals rather than looking to the past. We can make life simpler by looking for the purpose of our actions, rather than focusing on the cause. We should accept what is irreplaceable and have the courage to change what we can change. The book explains Adler's theories on teleology and that we should have a goal to change and develop, but to not need to strive to change to be special, but simply have the courage to be normal and happy, which also includes the courage to not worry about being disliked.

Kishimi and Koga (2017, p 90) believe there are *'two objectives for behaviour: to be self-reliant and to live in harmony with society'*. If we have accepted ourselves for who we are but want to become the best version of ourselves, then this is achieved through having purpose and having a goal, and that purpose can be found through a sense of community. When we are ready to change and find a purpose, we set ourselves goals and we develop. We can take control of our lives, realise that life can be simple, become happier and play a better part in our community.

The Maslow hierarchy model can be summed up by thinking about being stranded on a desert island and where you would focus your attention first. Even the painter, who luckily was swept ashore with his paints and brushes, may consider water and food and then shelter before sitting down to create a masterpiece. However, the painter might be motivated to paint first and Maslow appreciated that the model may not be followed in order.

Maslow's model can highlight motivations. He considered that people's needs change once they are satisfied at a certain level. He wrote:

> *It has been pointed out above several times that our needs usually emerge only when more prepotent needs have been gratified. Thus, gratification has an important role in motivation theory. If you deliberately plan on being less than you are capable of being, then I warn you that you'll be unhappy for the rest of your life.*
>
> (Maslow, 1943, p 370)

Flow

The coach and coachee discussing 'flow' may also help with considering how the coachee can be helped to remain motivated. Mihaly Csíkszentmihályi (2001) (famous for happiness studies) looked at achieving best performance though achieving the state of flow. He said people who learned to control inner experience would be able to determine the quality of their lives, and that this was as close as any of us could come to being happy. This emphasises the notion that individuals who learn to harness their motivation and achieve a state of flow, where they are fully immersed in and focused on an activity, can experience greater fulfilment and happiness in their lives.

Csíkszentmihályi said flow was *'a state in which people are so involved in an activity that nothing else seems to matter; the experience is so enjoyable that people will continue to do it even at great cost, for the sheer sake of doing it'* (Oppland, 2016). Flow is a highly focused state conducive to productivity, in which a person runs their best race, paints an incredible picture or achieves their best performance, when they are not fully aware of time or what else is going on around them, apart from the task at hand.

Stephen Kotler (2014) looks at the idea of flow in the context of extreme sportsmen in his book *The Rise of Superman: Decoding the Science of Ultimate Human Performance*. For Kotler, flow is the ultimate performance achieved from adrenaline rush situations. Kotler describes Csíkszentmihályi's list of ten factors required for flow to be achieved: clear goals, intrinsic motivation, concentration, absorption, lack of self-consciousness, time dilation, empowerment, direct feedback, immediate feedback and a balance between skills and challenge.

Kotler (2014) believes the amazing energises, and his book is filled with incredible feats performed by extreme sports stars in flow. He describes the skateboarder Danny Way who created a huge ramp and managed to fly over the Great Wall of China despite having a broken ankle: *'Enjoyment appears at the boundary between boredom and anxiety, when the challenges are just balanced with the person's capacity to act'* (Csíkszentmihályi, 2001, p 52). The coachee could consider whether they have achieved flow and what factors contributed to it, and this may help with their motivation and progress towards achieving their goal.

Bernstein (2019) also discusses motivation and maintains that motivation comes from vision: *'a clear destination that you desire with all your heart. Motivation is something you experience when you're connected to your vision'*. The 1989 Kevin Costner film *Field of Dreams* is famous for the quote *'If you build it, they will come'*. In *Field of Dreams*, Ray (portrayed by Costner) takes the first step to creating a baseball diamond by cutting the corn on his land. He sets things in motion to achieve what he desires. The quote is about faith and focus, and taking a step towards bringing something into your reality. Gabrielle Bernstein (2019) talks about bringing things into your reality in her book *Super Attractor*. She believes you should relax and trust that what you desire is on the way.

The coachee should realise the importance of motivation. Self-determination theory says that with individuals equal on ability and knowledge, motivation is the point of difference:

Encouragement = intrinsic motivation + extrinsic motivation

Reflection

The final stage is the Reflection stage. It involves reflection on progress and reviewing and improving goals when necessary. It involves reflection after achieving the goal, and lessons learned before embarking further on the coaching cycle and setting future goals. John Dewey famously said, *'We do not learn from experience ... we learn from reflecting on experience.'* It is important that reflection occurs on the goals and their progress, and on the coaching session, and if coaching is for appraisals, it should occur on the appraisal system and its success too.

Reflection-in-action and reflection-on-action

Schön's (1983) theory on reflection considers reflection-in-action and reflection-on-action. The coachee can be guided to reflect while they are actioning their plan, and to consider what they are doing as they do it, and whether they need to amend their actions.

When reflecting-on-action, the coachee can be reflecting on their goals, and several key elements can be considered to gain valuable insights and enhance the goal-attainment process. This includes reflection on their goal, reflection on progress, reflection on their plan, reflection on their growth and reflection to help them consider future plans and future goals.

Reflection on the goal can occur during the process of achieving the goal and afterwards. The coachee may want to consider their progress and be flexible regarding whether it is still the right goal and whether it is aligned, and make changes if required. Goals can be aligned with values, passions and a long-term vision, and can also be aligned with an organisation's goals. Goals that are in line with core values are more likely to be fulfilling and sustainable. The environment of the coachee may be changing and the coachee will need to ensure that their goal is still aligned and relevant, and to be aware of whether the priority of different goals is still correct.

It is important that the coachee reflects on the progress towards their goal and ensures they are still on track. They can reflect on their progress and celebrate small achievements to maintain motivation and a positive mindset. They can also reflect on their motivations and consider whether they are suitably motivated, as well as supported and encouraged by others. Another area to consider is that the most memorable experiences, regardless of whether they were positive or negative, will help the formation of future plans.

The coachee can also be helped to reflect on the plan itself and assess whether the initial action plan and strategies need adjustment based on the insights gained. They may need to reflect on the barriers to their progress and the time and resources required, and check that their plan is still the best way of achieving their goal; they should also be open to modifying their approach as needed.

The coach can suggest various tools for reflection. This might include adding self-assessment to their personal development plan, requesting feedback, making a mind-map, completing a SWOT analysis of themselves, surveys and comparing their pre- and post-coaching experiences. The coachee could write a case study on their experience to help support the development of a coaching culture.

Flexibility

Adam Grant (2016), the author of *Originals: How Non-Conformists Change the World*, writes about the need for reflection. The coachee might need to reflect and be flexible with plans. Grant also believes focus on achievement motivation can crowd out originality:

> *The more you value achievement, the more you come to dread failure. If we are to ever come up with anything original, then we will probably need to learn from failure along the way.*
>
> (Grant, 2016, p 10)

Grant comments on many aspects of achieving success through original thinking. These include his comments on generating multiple ideas, embracing diversity of thought, being open-minded and procrastinating. On the subject of idea generation, Grant comments that many believe that quality and quantity of ideas do not go hand in hand, but he found that *'when it comes to idea generation, quantity is the most predictable path to quality'*. Sir Richard Branson would probably agree with this, after creating success off the back of many failed business ideas. As Branson says, *'Business opportunities are like buses, there's always another one coming.'*

Grant believes in diversity and that

> *group think is the enemy of originality, people feel pressured to conform to the dominant default views instead of championing diversity of thought ... minority viewpoints are important not because they tend to prevail but because they stimulate divergent attention and thought.*
>
> (Grant, 2016, p 176)

Therefore 'jumping on the bandwagon' – a phrase coined in the nineteenth century from politicians lobbying using bandwagons – might not be the best idea; rather, the answer might be to have the courage to think critically. If the Thai football team, Panyee FC, had not had an original idea and the courage of their convictions, they would never have built their floating football pitch from old fishing rafts and gone on to become youth champions of Southern Thailand from 2004 until 2010.

Grant (2016) believes originality comes from being open-minded. He thinks having a 'beginner's mind' – or, as Buddhists call it, *shosin* – helps us to be original. This means being open and eager and having no preconceptions. This is the opposite of earned dogmatism, where research has shown that being recognised as an expert is linked with closed-mindedness, and being dismissive of others' viewpoints. It is very easy to find the flaws in an idea and to look at the problems or the reasons why an idea won't work. According to (Grant, 2016, p 165), *'when we use the logic of consequence, we can always find reasons not to take risks ... in the face of uncertainty our first instinct is often to reject novelty looking for reasons why unfamiliar concepts might fail'*. A coach can help the coachee to reflect and consider original goals and original plans for the future.

(Grant, 2016) believes in reflection and learning from mistakes. He also writes about procrastination, which *'may be the enemy of productivity but it can be a resource for creativity'* (Grant,

2016, p 95). He writes that procrastination provides us with *'time to generate novel ideas'* and *'keeps us open to improvisation'* (Grant, 2016, p 95). Grant believes that letting an idea evolve slowly helps it to develop better – but there is a balance. As George Bernard Shaw said, *'If you take too long in deciding what to do with your life, you'll find you've done it'*.

The coachee can also reflect on the lessons learned throughout the journey, and consider the new skills, knowledge or personal growth acquired in pursuit of the goal. They can reflect on their progress, achievements and lessons learned, and use this to help them set future goals.

Reflection on appraisal

Coaching should be used for appraisals. If a school has an embedded coaching culture, then the coaches leading appraisals should not only consider the goals of the individuals but also reflect on the success of the appraisal system. Even if the system is evaluated and appears successful, there will always be room for marginal gains and improvements to the system. The coach and coachee should both reflect on the appraisal system, and use the feedback to further improve coaching in appraisals for the future:

Reflection = Reviewing + Improving + Future goals

STAFF **TRAINING DISCUSSIONS**

- How important do you think it is to have choice of who you partner with in a coaching relationship?
- Do you think your organisation dedicates sufficient time and resources to coaching? How could they change this if not?

→

- Do you think it is important that appraisals are based on multiple sources of evidence? What do you think are the best forms of evidence?
- Do you think it is possible to set a goal when you do not have perspective on your performance? Explain your answer.
- Do you think the TEACHER model would help you to structure a coaching style conversation for an appraisal? Explain your answer.

> **COACHING 'BOOK CLUB' SUGGESTIONS**
>
> *Originals: How Non-Conformists Change the World* by Adam Grant. This book has stories from lots of different fields supporting original thinking, and includes interesting research like differences in behaviours due to sibling order. Using his own advice, I should write something a bit negative about myself, as apparently by sharing flaws it makes people appear more intelligent.
>
> *The 7 Habits of Highly Effective People* by Stephen Covey. Even if you do not want to read this book from a coaching perspective, I would urge you to read it if you are panicking about what your next assembly could be on, as this is a great resource.
>
> *Performance Coaching: The Handbook for Managers, HR Professionals and Coaches* by Angus McLeod. I really like the practical nature of this book, with some great tools and techniques and highlighted boxes, including 'linguistic tips'. This is another great book to develop your coaching skills.

Chapter 5:
IMPLEMENTING A COACHING CULTURE

> **LEARNING OBJECTIVES**
>
> - To examine the barriers to creating a coaching culture.
> - To know how to plan to overcome the barriers.
> - To consider the impact of coaching and how to evaluate it.

Creating the culture

Hawkins (2012) outlines an approach to developing a coaching culture that includes creating a coaching strategy, ensuring support from leaders, developing coaches and making coaching the predominant management style.

Developing a plan to implement coaching within an organisation requires a vision and a plan for managing change, which includes consideration of the barriers to change and a plan for adoption of changes. Communicating a vision that encapsulates coaching principles along with the values of the organisation is a good starting point.

Many educational bodies now support coaching in schools. The Independent Association of Prep Schools fully endorses coaching and believes coaching is an integral leadership skill. It supports members by delivering a fully funded Level 7 Coaching qualification to 24 serving heads every year, through its partnership with Charlie

Warshawski and his team from Love Your Coaching. The Heads Conference also delivers coaching for leadership courses. McBain et al (2015) conducted research involving 4500 managers, CEOs and HR directors, and highlighted the need for the commitment to development, starting at the top. Developing coaches at the top of an organisation is a strategy outlined by Anderson, Frankovelgia and Hernez-Broome (2016). They described this as seeding and being one of five strategies outlined as a finding from their study with 347 senior business leaders.

Coaching and leading learning organisations

Ries and Trout (2001) comment that positioning leads to an organisation's success. This is when a unique impression is left in a customer's mind that is desirable and different from others in the marketplace. People form images of organisations based on values, products and/ or services, business structures, ethics, reputation as an employer and legal compliance. People also form perceptions from associated publicity and whether the company is seen as a market leader – that is, they are positioned first in the customer's mind. Think about schools in your area and what they say about themselves, what others say about them and where they are trying to position themselves.

To be positioned top in people's minds, leading educational organisations need to be learning organisations embracing continuous improvement, which can be led by a total quality management (TQM) approach. TQM is about delivering high-quality products and/or services to maximise customer satisfaction, and is an organisation-wide effort towards continuous improvement. In a school, college or university, this means everyone is invested in doing their best.

Martinez-Lorente (1998, p 2) comments that Feigenbaum and Ishikawa are perhaps the greatest contributors to the development of the term TQM. *'The other recognised quality management gurus such as Crosby, Deming and Juan have shaped the dimensions, practices and mechanism which underpin the concept.'* TQM has historically been linked with industry in Japan, and *kaizen*, and the idea that efficiency evolves from small, incremental gains that add value. Deming's cyclical model of PDSA (plan-do-study-assess) is a tool of TQM, and the concept of planning, doing, studying and assessing can be implemented organisation-wide for marginal gains and continuous improvement of the entire organisation.

For the quality of education offered by an institution to be positioned first in people's minds, TQM is necessary and can be achieved by encouraging buy-in from all staff and students. This can be achieved by all within the organisation feeling empowered, that their voice is being heard, and that they are clear about the organisation's vision and have aligned their goals with it. Coaching helps TQM, but is everyone in your school clear on its vision and values?

Leadership and vision

One role of a senior leader is to correctly identify the vision and strategic objectives of an organisation, then to encourage alignment of the goals of others within the organisation. The process of alignment works all the way down to each individual, whether they are staff or students. TQM then empowers each individual to look at how they can make a difference and be coached to add their value and achieve their goals. If small improvements align with organisational goals, then a system of a top-down and bottom-up approach appears to work.

Syed (2019) writes about Hirsh (2009) and strategies for focusing on why, what and how development occurs. Communicating the vision needs to be accompanied by the reasons for why, what and how growth is necessary and coaching is required.

Leadership styles and leader coaches

There are various leadership theories, including contingency, paternalistic, democratic and transformative. Kurt Lewin identified the styles of autocratic, democratic and laissez-faire leadership styles (Lewin et al, 1939). James Macgregor Burns (2010) helped to develop the idea of transformational leadership, where the leadership style relies on intrinsic motivation. Transformational leaders are charismatic and visionary, and they encourage their team members to embrace the leader's vision and mission. Burns' *Leadership* states that *'transformational leadership occurs when one or more persons engage with others in such a way that leaders and followers raise one another to higher levels of motivation and morality'* (quoted in Lee, 2014).

Tannenbaum and Schmidt (1958) developed a *'continuum of leadership behaviour'*, which was developed further in 1973. This involves four stages, referred to as *'tells, sells, consults, and join'*. The tells style is where the leader has an autocratic style and makes decisions on their own and the sells style is where the leader still retains control of the decision-making process but takes time to explain and promote their thinking to the team. The consults style is where the leader values the opinions of the team and the decision-making is a consultative process and the joins style is where the leader identifies issues for the team and the decision-making is a joint process.

The coaching leadership style goes beyond the consult stage and emphasises empowering team members through coaching principles. The leader adopts a coaching approach, actively listening to team members' ideas and concerns, asking powerful questions, providing support and helping team members develop their skills and reach their full potential. The coaching leader focuses on fostering a learning environment and building strong relationships with the team to achieve collective goals. Although coaching leadership and transformational leadership are different, they have many similarities and a powerful leader could be a transformational leader coach.

Leadership coach skills

Leaders require a range of skills and characteristics to help them perform their jobs effectively. Nobody ever described leadership as being easy. Ben Horowitz (2014) talks about hard things in his book *The Hard Thing About Hard Things*, building a business when there are no easy answers. Hard things can be hard for many reasons: because they involve a lot of thinking to gain clarity and certainty on a decision; because they require time and effort; or because they are linked with emotions. Horowitz mentions various leadership traits, including communication and transparency, and discusses how effective communication is vital for leaders to build trust, align teams and share the vision of the organisation. The book emphasises the importance of transparent communication, especially during challenging times.

Another factor mentioned is emotional intelligence (EQ) and the emotional toll that leadership responsibilities can take on individuals (Goleman, 2020). Leaders with high EQ can better understand and manage their own emotions and those of their teams, fostering a positive and supportive work environment. EQ profoundly impacts service to others and communication. Leaders with high EQ can empathise with individuals, understand their needs and provide compassionate and personalised service. Additionally, EQ enhances communication skills, enabling leaders to engage in active listening, express emotions effectively and navigate challenging conversations with sensitivity, fostering clear and empathetic communication. High EQ leads to more effective coaching.

In his book *Everybody Matters*, Bob Chapman (2016) explains how conscious leaders run conscious businesses and realise the importance of looking after individuals. If an individual is performing well, it can help the performance of a team, and if a team is performing well, it can help the performance of the business. The British Army, celebrated for its leadership, has the motto 'Serve to Lead' at the Royal Military Academy in Sandhurst. Coaching leaders need to be team players and have strong collaborative skills, and they also need to realise the importance of serving others.

To adopt a leadership coach approach, leaders need to be strong communicators, which includes being good listeners. Leaders need to be able to hold coaching conversations, but they also need to be role models and have the humility to seek feedback and be open to being coached. Leaders need to try to develop a wide range of communication skills, including the ability to ask powerful questions but also be an empathetic communicator. They would need to be an active listener, and be aware of their non-verbal cues and body language. They would need to be able to offer respectful but constructive feedback and be encouraging, motivating and supportive.

Barriers to implementing a coaching culture

Elisabeth Kübler-Ross (1969) created a model illustrating reactions to change in terms of morale and confidence over time. She described the stages as moving through shock, denial, frustration, depression, experiment, decision and integration. This curve could apply to individuals or teams being introduced to coaching, but also to some extent to the organisation's attitude to developing a coaching culture. If you think about your own experience in education, you may feel as if you have experienced this. Maybe this encapsulated your feelings towards virtual or hybrid teaching and learning.

If an organisation is to implement a coaching culture, then one of the first steps is to identify the barriers to its implementation, in order to better support people though their different reactions in response to the change. Tahir (2019) describes resistance to change as including:

> *fear of uncertain future, previous failure of change initiatives, old habits of employees, living in comfortable zone, hostility among employees, employees' unions, strict bureaucratic structures and organisational culture.*

Smale (2014) describes the work of Ehrich and Hansford in the *A–Z Coaching Handbook*. The barriers include incorrect matching of coaches and learners, a lack of top-down support and resentment felt by those not involved in the scheme and the perception of favouritism. In terms of leadership, the barriers could be conflicting leadership approaches and a lack of support.

One solution is for senior leaders to invest in coaching and to be role models, and to model coaching approaches. This could be further supported by leaders gaining coaching qualifications and being open to coaching others, and being coached themselves. Leaders can work with others to develop a vision for coaching within the organisation. Leaders can commit time to developing others as part of the strategic development plan, and praise and reward managers who commit to developing others. Further barriers for leadership include a threat to organisational structure, and motivation and tolerance to change. A solution is communicating clearly on perceived threats and developing a strategy for change. This is further explained by effective communication of a coaching strategy and its effect on organisational structure, supported by individual coaching so coaches are aware of their own perceptions of threat. Leaders could encourage a champion versus challenger approach, encouraging reasons for change to counteract those who are against, encourage experimentation and embrace failure as a tool for learning. A further barrier for leadership is a lack of transparency and trust. Trust can be developed by leaders being open to feedback and a commitment to develop openness and working relationships.

In terms of coaching, further barriers include skills, relationships, recognition and approach. A solution to a lack of coaching skills it to create opportunities for training on coaching, and to practise and reflect on coaching. External coaches could also be employed. Senior leaders can also communicate the impact of coaching within organisations. Relationships can also be a barrier to coaching. A solution is to contract coaching conversations and to consider relationships when pairing coach and coaches. Leaders can overcome the barrier of recognition of coaching by praising coaching success, and also praising and promoting good caching practice.

Another barrier to coaching is the approach and the adoption of complicated techniques. Coaches will all have different approaches to their conversations, but models add structure to conversations. The TEACHER model helps to develop a coaching culture in schools as it can be used by students and teachers alike. The adoption of the same model by all should enable an easier adoption of a coaching culture.

Lack of resources can be another barrier. Senior leaders can help overcome this barrier by investing in coaching and evaluating its impact so return on investment is considered.

At the level of each individual, barriers might be fear of failure and lack of confidence, and perceived threats. These can be overcome by the organisation developing growth mindsets and encouraging a culture of learning from mistakes and coaching to develop confidence. Leaders should consider change-management models when implementing the coaching culture.

Plan for adopting change for a coaching culture

In his book on leadership, John Kotter (2012) describes an eight-step change model:

1. create urgency;
2. build coalition;
3. form vision and initiatives;
4. enlist volunteers;
5. remove barriers;
6. generate wins;
7. sustain acceleration;
8. institute change.

Prosci, a company involved in change management solutions, created its own model for change called the ADKAR change model, which focuses on awareness, desire, knowledge, ability and reinforcement. Following is a five-step model combining Kotter's (2012) model and the Prosci ADKAR model (Prosci, 2023), including reference to climate, collaboration, communication, goals and embedding.

Climate

The first stage is climate. Stakeholders need to be made aware of the climate. In the Prosci ADKAR model (Prosci, 2023), the first element is raising awareness of why the change is necessary and the risks of not embracing the change. Early communication promoting the benefits of change and the reasons for the change is important in order to build desire for change. According to Kotter (2012), urgency needs to be created regarding why it has to happen now. PESTLE and SWOT analyses can help support communication on climate. In schools, this might be in relation to the skills gap that is reported for our future workforces or response to advancing technologies. It would be important to communicate what coaching looks like in the organisation, and how and when coaching would be used by staff and students.

Collaboration

The second stage is collaboration. It is important to demonstrate leadership with a clear vision and a business case for change, in accordance with Kotter's third step, but it also requires consideration of the resources required, in line with Kotter's second step for a 'coalition' to be formed of other effective change leaders in order to support all individuals. Resources need to be considered early, so any that are necessary are in place – including people – before the change is instigated. This might include collaboration from the human resources department. Discussions are required about which members of the organisation will be drivers of the change and the building of a team, and communication to change leaders on their involvement in the collaboration. The collaboration will mean a successful plan can be developed that considers implications at the leadership, managerial, team and individual levels, ensuring alignment of these goals. In schools, this might initially be decisions on budgets for coaching, and then it might include decisions on whether there is employment of external business coaches or instructional coaches, or a budget for training and qualifications. Another factor would be the time allocated to coaching. Coaching would need to be a focus on the whole-school development plan. An initial team that is responsible and accountable for implementing a coaching culture, that works on the vision, the plan and its progress, would be required.

Communication

The third stage of supporting change is communication. This means providing an outlet for listening to concerns as people move through different stages of the change cycle, and being empathetic and considering mental models and bias when handling people concerned with change. This might be hearing about further barriers that need to be addressed. These outlets might be developed on a group or individual basis. Kotter (2012) describes removing obstacles, and as part of the communication the process of change needs to be explained, including timelines and how the change will affect the organisation. This might include communications released at different times regarding how coaching will develop teachers and support staff, and how it will help develop students. The Prosci ADKAR Model (Prosci, 2023) details knowledge on how to change (what to do during the transition), and knowledge on how to perform effectively in the future state (knowledge on the ultimate skills and behaviours needed to support the change). It is not only important to create forums for discussions of change but also to communicate feedback on change following these discussions. Communications need to be developed in supporting teams and individuals on what coaching is, how to coach and what good coaching conversations look like.

Goals

The next stage is goals. The Prosci ADKAR Model (Prosci, 2023) states that desire needs to be created. This can be achieved through goal-setting. Kotter (2012) explains how short-term goals also need to be planned in order for further desire to be generated from small wins. Support needs to be in place to help individuals and teams set goals. Individuals will need support as they trial small changes and demonstrate Prosci's 'ability'. According to Prosci (2023), there may be a large gap between knowledge and ability, and to ensure that in addition to training to impart knowledge, employees are given sufficient tools to build their own ability. Skills or knowledge gaps need to be identified in order to create effective goals. People need to know what changes will be made and the options to make them. Goals can be developed for students, teaching staff and support staff that align with the overall vision of the organisation, including long- and short-term goals for small wins. In a school, these goals might be gaining coaching qualifications; completing coaching courses; attending coaching inset; an appraiser coaching an appraisee; coaching a new teacher to the profession or a new member of staff to the school; pupils learning about coaching; parent communications released on coaching; pupils peer coaching each other; or teachers coaching in lessons.

Embedding

The final stage is embedding. This is Kotter's (2012) final stage, where changes are anchored in corporate culture and this is achieved through recognition. For the change to be fully embedded, it will need to be reviewed and developed. The reviewing should be a regular process so there can be continuous improvements on areas requiring development. This helps to reinforce and sustain the acceleration of the change. For coaching to be embedded in an educational institution, it would need to be evident in all areas and be a term understood by all stakeholders. Embedding coaching in all areas would not be sufficient, and it would need to be practised regularly in all areas to be fully embedded. The TEACHER coaching model can be used to support all involved in all areas of educational organisations.

Measuring coaching impact

A coaching approach is not something that should be entered half-heartedly. A coaching approach and the philosophy behind it include happiness; motivation; productivity; performance; reflection; growth mindset; autonomy; and the importance of relationships. What is there not to like? It needs to be lived and breathed in an organisation. Coaching approaches need to be fully embedded.

There are multiple ways in which coaching can be embedded in an organisation using the TEACHER coaching model. Coaching impacts can include increased skills or knowledge, which might be reactively simple to record and monitor. However, other success criteria might include the learning experience, employee happiness, cultural impact, efficiency impact and financial impact, where it might be harder to monitor the impact within the organisation. Bansal and Tripathi (2017) comment on how analysis of training is often not completed. In exploring and monitoring context, the Warr, Bird and Rackham (1970) CIRO evaluation model can be used to measure the effect. CIRO stands for Content, Input, Reaction and Outcome. It is a training evaluation model used to assess the effectiveness of training and development programmes. How often have you been asked after a training session what you thought of the content, how well the resources – such as time, money and effort – were invested in the training program, and what the participants' reactions were to the training programme. Did they find the training valuable, engaging and relevant to their needs? What changes or improvements have been observed in participants' knowledge, skills, behaviour and performance as a result of the training? Did the training achieve the desired learning objectives and outcomes? This is usually ascertained in the form of a quick questionnaire returned at the end of the training.

The CIRO model can be used to look at intermediate and ultimate objectives and consider the alignment and whether an individual's benefit from coaching has a subsequent improved impact on the organisation. The Anderson Value of Learning model (Anderson et al, 2016) can also be considered. This has three stages: alignment of training against strategic priorities for the organisation; using a range of methods to assess and evaluate the contribution of learning; and establishing the most relevant approaches. In a school, it is important to reflect on the overall impact of coaching for its input into the strategic development plan, and monitoring developments and their alignment with the overall vision. The Anderson model shows that different approaches are required for different areas to be evaluated.

People's responses to being coached can be measured. A study including 100 coaches by Hicks, Carter and Sinclair (2013) found a statistically significant rise in employee perception of wellbeing from being coached. When considering people's reactions as a measurement of success for coaching implementation, various models suggest its measurement. Methods of evaluating training are described by Spearhead Training (www.spearhead-training.co.uk/blog/evaluating-training). The Kirkpatrick evaluation model and the Phillips model both suggest measuring reactions. The Kirkpatrick Model (Businessballs, 2021) is a widely used framework for evaluating the effectiveness of training and development programs. It was developed by Donald L Kirkpatrick in the 1950s and has since become a standard in the field of training evaluation. The model consists of four levels of evaluation: reaction, learning, behaviour and results. The Phillips Return on Investment Model consists of five levels of evaluation: assessing participants' reactions to the training; measuring the extent of learning and skill acquisition; evaluating the application of learning in the workplace; examining the impact of the training on specific business outcomes; and quantifying the financial return on investment by comparing monetary benefits to training costs. These models allow organisations to assess training effectiveness from immediate reactions to long-term financial results, aiding in data-driven decision-making and resource allocation. Kaufman's model is also a comprehensive framework for training evaluation. It includes five levels of assessment, ranging from identifying performance needs to measuring the impact of the training on organisational performance. The Kaufman model also suggests evaluating reactions to input – for example, evaluating training resources and process separately. This could take the form of Likert scales or happy face surveys; it could be informal or formal feedback; or Brinkerhoff's (2018) Success Case Method could be used to identify and review the most and least successful areas of coaching. There could be individual surveys on input and process at the end of a coaching period, or agreed and recorded reflections on coaching from all involved.

The learning achieved following a coaching approach can also be measured. Kirkpatrick's and Phillips' models both evaluate learning. Kaufman's model similarly looks at acquisition of skills and knowledge. This could include the use of surveys and pre- and post-coaching surveys. Gamification could also be used and coaching course certification recorded. Interviews and records of achievement could also document success from coaching. In schools, the Microsoft Learn platform is excellent for accessing online courses and enjoying gamification, Microsoft has also introduced a coaching course. Staff members can share links so their progress can be monitored. Microsoft Forms also allow an easy way to engineer surveys on coaching.

Behaviour changes can also be evaluated following the implementation of a coaching culture. Kirkpatrick's level three is about evaluating behaviour and Kaufman describes this as application, and Phillips as application and implementation. Evaluations can be achieved through self-assessment questionnaires, peer surveys, through informal feedback, focus groups, work observation, customer surveys and comment and from KPIs. Microsoft Forms provides another useful tool for surveys and for providing insights into overall results.

The effectiveness of coaching can be monitored for individual impact and results, and again the CIRO model can be useful at an individual level. Microsoft Excel or Power BI can be used to analyse progress, or for use as a Gantt chart for monitoring progress against KPIs. A Gantt chart in Microsoft Excel can be created by listing the tasks, start dates and durations in separate columns. The same applies to monitoring organisational impacts. However, organisational impacts can also be monitored by monitoring learning and development metrics, including numbers of people undergoing and completing training, and surveys on morale. The NHS commissioned a report to evaluate the impact of its coaching through the Institute of Employment Studies. This report, by Carter et al (2018), focused on the coaching culture at the NHS and the development of accredited coaches and the provision of services from external coaches. The NHS report followed a qualitative approach with results based predominantly on telephone interviews. Another initiative was for coaches and coaches to write a learning vignette based on their conversation and their outcomes. The findings of interviews of a coachee by someone other than their coach, or short documentations of case studies, could help to support the case for coaching in schools.

Return on investment (ROI), which is Phillips' fifth level of evaluation, is harder to monitor. ROI is the cost of the coaching divided by the benefit and can be shown in leaders and mangers' reports. It has been recognised for many years that a methodology for measuring its impact is necessary (Schlosser, Flynn and Heiskell, 2007).

Although not all organisations quantify their ROI on investment from coaching programmes, Renton (2009) discusses the example from a North American hotel chain that invested in an ROI study and found its coaching programmes to have a value of 221 per cent. Renton also mentions the intangible impacts of coaching, including *'better commitment, better teamwork, better job satisfaction, and better customer service and communication'* (Renton, 2009, p 150).

Kaufman's fifth level is about evaluating impact for customers and the society as a whole. A theory of change is a systematic and visual representation of how a desired change is expected to happen. It outlines the relationships between various activities, inputs, outputs and outcomes to achieve a specific goal or impact. School managers and leaders can create reports for external communications or with governors, using a theory of change model to add structure to the report.

Evidence of success of coaching in appraisals

Coaching to facilitate change and improvement should be evident in all areas of a school if a coaching culture is embedded. Coaching can be a very successful tool for use in teacher appraisals. There has been considerable research on the success of coaching style appraisals and coaching for professional development.

Hollweck (2019) published an interesting study using data from surveys, interviews, focus groups and teacher documentation. The study was conducted with the Western Quebec Schools Board in Canada. The study found that coaching relationships with teacher coaches and teachers led to *'positive emotion, engagement, positive relationships, meaning and accomplishment'* (p 6) but the quality of the coaching relationship was also a key factor. However, Hollweck found that this positive benefit was for the coach. The feeling of well-being for a coach is often reported, and is one area to consider in the success of coaching in schools.

One of the most comprehensive studies was performed by Kraft et al (2018) who conducted an analysis of 60 studies of teacher coaching. They found coaching to have a large positive effect on teachers' practice, and also a positive effect, although smaller, on student achievement. Their study was based predominantly in the United States and other developed countries. Their research did, however, question whether coaching was better implemented in smaller scale targeted programs.

There have also been studies on the benefits of peer coaching amongst student teachers based on 8 studies in the United States and New Zealand. Lu (2010) found the effects of peer coaching to be that of improved emotional support, and increased professionalism. Although these benefits were reported, the studies also confirmed that the effects of coaching were related to the quality of the coaching, further supporting the need for coaching knowledge and experience for teachers.

In a further study by van Nieuwerburgh et al (2020) where the quality of the coaching was deemed consistently good, the study looked at the effects of coaching on 14 aspirational school leaders in Australia. Although the sample was small, the results showed that teachers reported their experiences of coaching as positive. The study concluded that coaching resulted in positive emotions, people feeling safe to explore, having time to reflect and focusing on what they valued as important.

In summary, these studies collectively affirm the key role of coaching in schools, and the need for a coaching culture to drive positive change. Highlighting its success in teacher appraisals and professional development, the research underscores that the impact of coaching extends across various aspects of education. Findings from diverse studies demonstrate the positive influence of coaching on emotions, engagement, relationships and accomplishment. Overall, these insights call for the widespread integration of coaching practices, with an emphasis on enhancing coaching quality to meet the unique needs of teachers.

To prove the impact of coaching in appraisals in a school, Brinkerhoff's (2018) Success Case Method could be used. This has five steps: planning a success case study; defining what success should look like through drafting an 'impact model'; writing a survey that identifies best-case and worst-case scenarios; then implementing this survey, documenting success cases and conducting interviews, drawing conclusions, writing recommendations and communicating findings to stakeholders. This could be done by gathering evidence from individual coaches and coachees before and after a set of coaching conversations, or it could be used by senior leaders to consider the impact of coaching in all appraisals across the organisation. Sparrow (2007) discusses Passmore's integrative coaching model, and how another method is asking the coachee to write a *'change balance sheet'*.

Jonah Berger's (2013) book *Contagious: How to Build Word of Mouth in the Digital Age* explores the science behind why certain ideas, products or content become viral and spread rapidly in society. The book highlights six key principles that contribute to the contagiousness of ideas. These principles are referred to as the STEPPS framework. Although the model was not designed for this purpose, it could be used to write a case study to promote coaching.

- **S** stands for social currency – through sharing their story, the coachee may feel socially valuable.
- **T** is for triggers, considering how the case study could be written so people are triggered to keep sharing their story.
- **E** for emotion – which should be conveyed through the personal account, prompting people to share content more readily.

- **P** for public – making the study easily observable or visible.
- **P** is for practical value – contagious ideas often provide practical value to people's lives.
- **S** for stories – people love stories and narratives that are relatable and engaging.

Using STEPPS for writing coaching case studies may help make the coaching culture 'contagious'.

A coaching culture is about enlightenment and reflection. An organisation embedding coaching would need to reflect on its approach, and through enlightenment, evaluate its benefit. There should be a coaching cycle where the culture continues to improve.

STAFF TRAINING DISCUSSIONS

- Are you a leader? If so, what type of leadership style do you favour? Do you think you could be a transformational leader coach? Could others in your organisation?
- Do you think all staff goals are aligned with the organisational goal? If not, how could using the TEACHER model help?
- How could using the TEACHER coaching model help to make staff happier and also help them perform better?
- How do you measure the impact of your teacher appraisals? If you conducted appraisals using the TEACHER model, how would you try to measure its impact?

COACHING 'BOOK CLUB' SUGGESTIONS

Emotional Intelligence: Why It Can Matter More Than IQ by Daniel Goleman. Whether you are coaching for soft skills, or just want to learn more about EQ, this is a must read. This book not only explains EQ but helps you improve your own EQ.

Leading Change by John Kotter. If you really do want more detail about how you can implement change and bring more coaching into your organisation, then this book and its model for change will help you form your plan.

Chapter 6:
BEING A COACH

> **LEARNING OBJECTIVES**
>
> - To help you understand the skills required of a coach, including communication skills, active listening and the Hofstede model.
> - To understand the relevance of cultural and individual differences.
> - To understand the boring but important bits about coaching, such as statements of ethics.

Role of a coach

Sir John Whitmore, author, racing car driver and coach, said the role of the coach was *'helping people liberate themselves from their fears to unlock the unlimited potential that most individuals possess'* (Renton, 2009, p 73). Kimsey House et al (2011, p 128) describe the role as to

> *challenge clients to pursue their fulfilment in spite of the circumstances – in spite of the voices all around them offering bad advice and contrary agendas and in spite of the clients own inner voice.*

Coaching to unlock potential and to help a coachee pursue fulfilment is a skill like any other, which will improve with practice. These two definitions offer a glimpse into the push–pull relationship of a coaching conversation and the balance of challenge and support. For a coach to be able to offer the correct balance, they need to be a good communicator. An inexperienced coach may need greater structure to their conversations, and to have considered the questions they may use in advance, whereas an experienced coach may be able to move seamlessly from coaching different individuals and make the conversation flow more naturally. The TEACHER model attempts to offer structure.

In addition to considering a model, coaches need many skills and tools to be effective. The tools can include using cards, role-play and different activities. Many activities are described in this book, but hundreds more are found online. However, the skills of the coach are arguably more important than the activities.

Coaches need to be humble. Jim Collins (2001), the author of *Good to Great*, describes leaders and humility in his book. The same can be said about the requirement for coaches to have humility and appreciation for others. He describes a leader looking out of a closed window and not seeing their reflection and embarking on self-appreciation, but rather looking through the glass at their team. The coach's focus is the coachee and how they can best help them.

A coach requires many skills and behaviours. These include communication skills, empathy, using feedback, curiosity and a respect for cultural differences. Before starting to practise coaching, the potential coach needs to be self-aware and consider these skills, and also be aware of the need for sensitivity.

The requirement for sensitivity and confidentiality

Sensitivity and confidentiality are important for the coach in their relationships with their clients. If clients are going to change, they need to be able to open up, and this needs to be done *'without fear that the information will be passed on without their approval'* (Ennis and Otto, 2015, p 31). Without confidentiality, there is no trust and *'the coaching will be tentative and there will be always an undercurrent of wonder about what is possibly being withheld'* (Kimsey-House et al, 2011, p 17).

Hill (2019) warns that as important as confidentiality is not promising complete confidentiality in coaching relationships, as complete confidentiality cannot be guaranteed due to potential legal, organisational or well-being reasons that mean a disclosure is required.

To be able to have deep and personal conversations, the client needs to trust their coach, and a relationship of trust and self-belief is created through the coach having strong social skills and being sensitive towards their client. Without sensitivity to how the client is feeling or to their situation, there will be no rapport or trust, so the outcomes of the coaching and mentoring sessions will be minimal. Without confidentiality, there is unlikely to be disclosure, and once again there will be limited outcomes. When considering trust, the coach may also wish to develop a statement about ethics. Many coaches and mentors sign up to the Global Code of Ethics generated by the European Mentoring and Coaching Council (EMCC Global, 2020) to ensure trust and confidence are built up at the very start of their relationship through contracting.

Statement of ethics

The EMCC (EMCC Global, 2020) has devised a code of ethics for mentors, coaches and supervisors. This document contains the following headings: terminology; working with clients; professional conduct; excellent practice; and signatories. The code of ethics initially lays out a brief definition of the terminology used and a description of the importance of dates being discussed, the nature of the methodology, commitments and the environment.

The nature of the coaching relationship is then defined, along with the importance of boundaries within the relationship, including it not being romantic or sexual, and the consideration of conflicts of interest and exploitation. The confidential nature of the conversations is also outlined.

The code of topics also comments on ending the relationship, in terms of the planned duration and the right to end the relationship early. This could be in reference to offering different help, or from reaching the limit of experience. The procedures for transferring clients and complaints procedures are also mentioned.

The commitment to learning and development of the mentor or coach is detailed, including how they should be able to contribute to the development of coaching/mentoring, be able to reflect on the relationship and have a commitment to continued professional development. The code outlines how the coach should be suitably qualified, and conduct themselves professionally. The document includes specific mention of commitment to CPD in terms of increased self-awareness in relation to inclusion, diversity, technology and the latest developments in changing social and environmental needs.

Although compiled by the EMCC (EMCC Global, 2020), the code is a global document. Policies and procedures related to keeping, storing and disposing of records in line with the laws and agreements of particular countries need to be included, in addition to compliance with organisational policies and procedures. This may include safeguarding of children and vulnerable adults. The issue of ultimate social responsibility, over confidentiality, also needs to be addressed.

The International Coaching Federation (2021) has also released its own code of ethics, which arguably is presented in a clearer and more coherent format. Its code adheres to equally important values of professionalism, collaboration, humanity and equity. It covers very similar areas to the EMCC Global Code of Ethics. However, areas of note include mention of financial arrangements in the early sections of the code.

In terms of relationships and conflicts of interest, the code details conflicts of interests that may arise though holding multiple contracts. It also mentions how coaches should adhere to the philosophy of doing good versus avoiding bad. The nature of power in the relationship is also considered in terms of cultural, relational, psychological and contextual issues, and in addition to being aware of bias related to age, gender, race and so on, it pays particular mention to military status. Intellectual property is also mentioned in relation to confidentiality.

The ICF also included detailed complaints procedures, including links to its ethical conduct review for responding to alleged unethical practices or behaviour deviating from the established ICF Code.

Trust and honesty are detailed in the code of ethics, along with the requirement to accurately represent value, make no misleading claims and be mindful of bias and discrimination. It may be useful for any policies related to coaching use in schools to consider some of the areas raised in these codes, but the necessity may depend on whether internal or external coaches are being used.

Cultural differences in coaching

We have already discussed the story of the elephant and the three blind men that is often accredited to the thirteenth-century Persian poet, and Sufi master Rumi. It is the story of three blind men finding an elephant. The first feels its trunk and says he has found a snake; the second feels a leg and is sure he is feeling a tree; and the third blind man feels an elephant ear and is clear he is touching a fan. The three blind men argue over the elephant, as they all know what they are feeling. This story is told to highlight the importance of having perspective. A coach should be a good role model and demonstrate the ability to have perspective. They should also be able to guide the coachee to gain greater perspective. People can have vastly different interpretations of the same situation based on their individual experiences and perspectives. Perspective can also be considered in relation to different cultures. To effectively work with individuals from different cultural backgrounds, it is important to approach coaching conversations with an open mind, actively listen and seek to understand each coachee's unique perspective.

A 2018 study of cultural identity and well-being involving 662 German students considered the impact of peers as socialisation agents, and their impact on cultural identity. The study found that peers helped students embrace their mainstream, and cultural or heritage identity and that this had the effect of higher life satisfaction and positive outcomes (Vietze et al, 2019).

A further study in 2022 looked at Danish and Indian students and the effects of globalisation, and its impact on cultural identity, happiness and our drive for a sense of belonging. Differences were found between the relationship of cultural identity and happiness, and how ethnic identities can sometimes have a negative effect on happiness if they are perceived as inferior (Damkier et al, 2022). Individuals and organisations should make a genuine effort to understand and respect cultural differences, and actively to promote cross cultural understanding and communication. Molinsky (2013) writes on different approaches, and how attempts should be made to learn the cultural code to improve coaching across cultures.

Disregarding cultural differences, coachees will always prefer to feel they are being respected, validated and 'seen'. The phrase 'I see you' is a powerful expression of acknowledgement that is commonly used in African cultures. It is more than just a simple greeting: it carries a deeper meaning of understanding, acceptance and respect, and was used in the film *Avatar*. When someone says, 'I see you', they are communicating that they recognise and acknowledge the person's presence, thoughts, feelings and experiences. It is a way of showing that the person is seen, heard and valued. In many African cultures, the concept 'I see you' is rooted in the belief that all individuals are interconnected and that one's actions and words can have a profound impact on others. Saying 'I see you' is a way of expressing empathy, compassion and solidarity, and of affirming the interconnectedness of all people. A coach might be able to convey the same feeling without using this phrase.

The Hofstede model

Coaches may wish to consider further implications of cultural differences. The Hofstede model is widely used in organisations to help consider different cultures. It is a framework for cross-cultural communication developed by Dutch social psychologist Geert Hofstede (2010). The model consists of six dimensions that are used to compare and contrast cultural values and attitudes across different countries and regions. The six dimensions are: power distance; individualism versus collectivism; masculinity versus femininity; uncertainty avoidance; long-term orientation versus short-term orientation; and indulgence versus restraint. These six dimensions can all be considered in the context of coaching.

The first of the Hofstede (2010) dimensions is power distance. This refers to how individuals in a society accept unequal distribution of power and authority, and whether societies expect deference and obedience, or value equality more. Hierarchical societies are those with a significant power distance. Japan ranks highly on power distance, and there is a strong emphasis on hierarchy and respect for authority. In the age of the Samurai, the Shogun was the supreme leader. The Shogun, due to hierarchy, was protected by others, and always sat furthest from a door. In a Japanese meeting room, you may still be likely to see the person with the most authority positioned furthest from the door. As a coach, you may wish to consider the positioning, relative alignment and type of seating for a coaching conversation, and the messages they may be conveying to the coachee. While considering seating, it may be useful to consider whether the coachee comes from a contact or non-contact culture. This is a concept developed by American anthropologist Edward T Hall (1976). Contact and non-contact cultures refer to how comfortable people are within certain distances of each other – that is, their personal bubble – and how it alters for people they know and those they do not. Some contact cultures are comfortable approximately half a metre closer than those from non-contact cultures. An easy way around this may be to let the coachee choose where they sit, and invite them to feel free to move the chairs to make them feel more comfortable. A chair on wheels might be useful as the coach and coachee can then alter their distance and respective angles without any awkward chair scraping noises.

Although there are some exceptions, cultures with greater power distance often tend to be regarded as having a collectivist culture as opposed to an individualist culture. In individualist cultures, such as the United States, coaching typically focuses on individual achievement and self-improvement. Coaches may emphasise setting personal goals and taking ownership. In contrast, collectivist cultures such as Japan or China prioritise group harmony and cooperation. Coaches in these cultures may emphasise the importance of working together towards a shared goal, and placing the needs of the group above one's own needs. The United Kingdom is generally considered an individualist culture, although it has some collectivist tendencies. The outcome of the actions following a coaching conversation for appraisal should include personal development and improved performance for the organisation. As the coach guides the coachee to form their development goals, they should consider these two factors, and also consider the coachee's cultural inclination to individual and team goals.

Another dimension of the Hofstede (2010) model is masculinity–femininity, which refers to the degree to which a culture values traditionally 'masculine' traits such as assertiveness, competition and achievement, versus traditionally 'feminine' traits such as nurturing, collaboration and quality of life. Irrespective of gender, or how an individual identifies, or what their cultural background is, they may have a tendency to a particular set of traits. When coaching individuals from different cultural backgrounds, it is important to consider the masculinity–femininity dimension, as it can greatly influence the coachee's behaviour and values in the workplace. For example, individuals from cultures that place a high value on masculinity may be more focused on achieving results and individual recognition, while individuals from cultures that value femininity may prioritise collaboration and work–life balance. If you are coaching an individual from a culture that values 'feminine' traits, you may want to focus on developing their collaborative skills, and encourage them to seek out work–life balance. Conversely, if you are coaching an individual from a culture that values 'masculine' traits, you may want to focus on helping them to set challenging goals and developing their assertiveness, or you may just coach them to see things from the other perspective.

It may also be necessary to help the coachee gain perspective on how their cultural background and thoughts on gender might be affecting their relationships in the workplace. To help break down cultural gender stereotypes, a coach can raise awareness, challenge stereotypes, encourage diversity and lead by example. The coach should promote inclusive behaviour and attitudes, and may need to guide the coachee to improve their own ability to work effectively with people from different backgrounds.

A further dimension is uncertainty avoidance, and the degree in which cultures tolerate ambiguity and uncertainty. Cultures with high uncertainty avoidance tend to have strong rules and regulations, a low tolerance for risk and a preference for clear structures and procedures. In contrast, cultures with low uncertainty avoidance tend to be more flexible, comfortable with ambiguity and willing to take risks. Uncertainty avoidance can impact a coachee's willingness to take risks, be creative and adapt to change. Individuals from cultures with high uncertainty avoidance may feel uncomfortable with ambiguity, and prefer clear rules and procedures, while individuals from cultures with low uncertainty avoidance may be more open to ambiguity and experimentation.

If you are coaching an individual from a culture with high uncertainty avoidance – or, regardless of cultural differences, any individual with high uncertainty avoidance – you may want to provide clear guidelines and procedures, and focus on developing their comfort with structured processes. On the other hand, if you are coaching an individual with low uncertainty avoidance, you may want to encourage experimentation and creativity, and help them develop their ability to adapt to change and uncertainty. When a coach is helping a coachee to become more enlightened, they may wish to ask the coachee about their relationship with certainty.

Hofstede (2010) also recognised that some cultures have different relationships with time, and are more oriented towards long-term goals, while others are oriented towards shorter-term goals. Time orientation, or the ways in which individuals and cultures perceive and value time, is an important aspect to consider when coaching individuals from diverse cultural backgrounds. This is because different cultures have different attitudes towards time and punctuality, and may favour flexibility and adaptability over punctuality. This might be worth bearing in mind if the coachee turns up late for the coaching conversation – or this may just be that they work in a school, as I have done, where every single clock in the entire school appears to tell a different time!

The relationship with the value of time also affects the length of the goals. Cultures with a long-term orientation tend to focus on future rewards, delayed gratification and persistence in achieving goals. In contrast, cultures with a short-term orientation tend to prioritise immediate results and focus on the present moment. This does not mean the coach should consider the cultural background of the coachee and only set either long- or short-term goals, but it is important to recognise that the coachee's cultural background may affect their relationship with long- and short-term goals, and to support them to achieve either short- or long-term goals as required. The Swiss, Chinese and Japanese are considered to have a tendency to a longer-term goal orientation, while the British, Australians, Canadians and Americans are often more short-term focused.

The tendency for longer or shorter term goals is linked to the final dimension of the model, which is indulgence versus restraint. Indulgence refers to cultures that place a high value on gratifying immediate needs and desires, while restraint refers to cultures that place a higher value on self-discipline and controlling impulses. Cultural differences in indulgence versus restraint can impact coaching in various ways. Individuals from indulgent cultures may be motivated by immediate rewards, take more risks and prefer positive feedback, while individuals from restrained cultures may prioritise self-discipline, make more deliberate decisions and value critical feedback. As a coach, it is important to understand these cultural differences and tailor your approach accordingly, while still considering each individual's unique needs and goals. Differences in indulgence and restraint can also apply to coachees of different ages. Consider the experiment that Dr Robert Winston conducted in the television series *Child of Our Time*, based on the Stanford marshmallow experiment and delayed gratification in children, where children were allowed extra treats if they could wait. Considering indulgence and restraint tendencies is important for cultural and age differences.

The Hofstede (2010) model is useful for considering many aspects of cultural differences, but another model that could be applied is Edward T Hall's (1976) theory of culture, with its three dimensions of context, time and space. In addition to categorising cultures as being contact and non-contact cultures, Hall categorised cultures as being high- and low-context cultures. In low-context cultures, communication is often more direct, and relies more heavily on explicit language to convey meaning. These cultures may value individualism, transparency and efficiency. Examples of low-context cultures include the United States, Germany and Australia.

In contrast, in high-context cultures, communication is often more subtle and indirect. People may expect others to read between the lines and interpret messages, and communication relies heavily on implicit cues such as body language, tone of voice and cultural context to convey meaning. These cultures may value relationships, hierarchy and social harmony. Examples of high-context cultures include Japan, China and the Middle East. The use of metaphors is an important coaching tool, and may help build a relationship with the coach and coachee, particularly if they prefer indirect communication. An example of this would be describing a coachee's communication style as being like a game of chess; just as in chess, they would need to think several moves ahead and anticipate how their message will be received and interpreted by the other person. An experienced coach may be able to choose a metaphor best linked to the coachee – for example, a sporting metaphor for a sportsperson, or a nature metaphor for an environmentalist.

It may be easy for those in high- and low-context cultures who are communicating to be misinterpreted. One issue is that in low-context cultures, people may expect others to communicate more directly and explicitly, which can sometimes be perceived as blunt or lacking in nuance by those from high-context cultures. Active listening from the coach can help to gauge the level of direct or indirect communication that the coachee is using, enabling them to learn how to communicate best with them. This can apply regardless of culture.

The second area in Hall's theory of culture is time. In some cultures, time is viewed as a commodity that can be bought, sold and saved through the purchasing or selling of services and services, while in others time is seen as a more fluid and flexible concept that is not bound by strict schedules or deadlines. We have already discussed the effect of cultural background on punctuality, or lack thereof, and on the setting of long- and short-term goals, but we can also consider time in the context of communication. Different cultures have different relationships with pauses in communications. In Chinese culture, long pauses in a conversation are often seen as a sign of active listening – as a sign of thoughtfulness, respect and attentiveness – rather than as a sign of discomfort or disinterest. This is because in Chinese culture, there is a strong emphasis on the value of silence, particularly in social situations where it is important to show respect for others. It is also normal in Aboriginal cultures to have long periods of contemplative silence before responding. However, in other cultures there may be a preference for direct and assertive communication, and long pauses in a conversation may be seen as awkward or uncomfortable. In Latin America and the Middle East, there is often a greater emphasis on showing warmth and friendliness through communication. In these cultures, long pauses in communication may be viewed negatively, and may be misinterpreted as a sign of disapproval or rejection. This might be a useful skill to practise. You could try playing around with lengths of pauses in conversations. There will be a spectrum from where the pause becomes helpful to people potentially thinking you are a bit odd. You could try to work out optimum pause lengths and how you could help a coachee to become more comfortable with pauses, and time for reflection and consideration.

Another area to consider with respect to cultural differences in time orientation is deadlines. A coach and coachee may have a different approach to time and its value with respect to setting and keeping to deadlines. The coach will need to be mindful of this when helping the coach to develop SMART goals that are time related.

We have already discussed Hall's (1976) third dimension of space, and the differing personal space distances of different cultures. Some cultures are more comfortable with closer distances when communicating, and may also have a different relationship with touch during a conversation to express closeness or connection. I sometimes think I have a forcefield around me. If somebody goes to head for an elbow nudge with me (in a kind of Basil Brush boom-boom style), they end up going for an air nudge instead. However, it is worth considering that space can also extend to a person's belongings – for example, their car, their desk or their pen.

The idea of personal space can even stretch to a person's willingness to share personal stories. In many Indigenous cultures around the world, storytelling is a deeply valued tradition and an important way of passing down cultural knowledge and history. Sharing personal stories can also be a way of building relationships and strengthening bonds. In Iran, Iraq and Saudi Arabia, people also often share personal stories and experiences as a way to demonstrate their hospitality and to show welcome. By understanding and respecting cultural differences in space, coaches can help build trust and rapport with coachees from diverse backgrounds.

Everybody is different, and cultural norms may not be relevant to the coachee if they do not conform to cultural stereotypes or expectations. Coaches need to understand and respect differences in their coachees, and adapt their approach to meet the unique needs and perspectives of their coachees.

Feedback

Many of Hall's and Hofstede's ideas can be applied when giving feedback in a coaching conversation. For instance, how hierarchy is seen within a culture might influence the coaching relationship, and the seniority of the person giving feedback. Coaches do not need to be older or more experienced than their coachee, but it is worth noting how different cultures might interpret the relative seniority and experience.

Andy Molinsky (2013) discusses the nature of feedback in different cultures. He notes that Germans like concise, constructive feedback, while the Chinese like gentler feedback with more positive reinforcement. The French are often more comfortable than other nations with criticising passionately. Although coaching is about guiding conversations, and not adopting a telling approach, the stating of disagreement can have implications in different cultures. Rebecca Knight (2015) describes how saying 'I disagree' in Asia can be seen as very aggressive, while saying it in France or Russia might be seen as an opportunity to build a relationship. Different cultures will have different cultural norms around feedback and praise, criticism and self-improvement, and coaches need to navigate these differences.

Non-verbal communication

While giving feedback and at other stages in the coaching conversation, it is also important to consider cultural differences in non-verbal communication. There are so many cultural differences in body language that a coach could not be expected to know all of them but should just try to raise their awareness. This can be linked to something as small as a nod of the head, which to Bulgarians and Greeks means no and not yes. Sitting cross-legged can cause issues too, as in Japan it may be seen as disrespectful, while showing the soles of your feet in India would be classed as rude. There are also cultural differences in use of eye contact. While eye contact in Great Britain could demonstrate active listening in a conversation, unbroken eye contact can be seen as aggressive and confrontational in other cultures. Active listening is also demonstrated in Sweden by the crossing of arms, while other cultures might see this as being closed and disinterested. Coaches can be mindful of these differences, and can try to use non-verbal communication to build rapport and trust with individuals from different cultures.

One way in which coaches can use non-verbal communication to build a relationship is through mirroring. Mirroring is a technique used in communication that involves reflecting the behaviour, body language or speech of another person. Mirroring can be done in a variety of ways, such as by matching the tone or pace of the other person's speech, using similar gestures or facial expressions, or adopting a similar posture. When done effectively, mirroring can help to establish trust and build a sense of rapport with the other person, as it can signal that the other person is being heard and understood. Research by Sanchez-Burks, Blount and Bartel (2009) focused on the differences between US Anglos and US Latinos in their responses to being mirrored. They found that US Latinos were more affected than US Anglos by whether mirroring occurred or not. It is possible that some cultures may view non-verbal mirroring as inappropriate or disrespectful, particularly if it is done in an exaggerated or insincere way. In some cultures, direct or overt displays of emotion may be seen as inappropriate or unprofessional, and mirroring may be perceived as an attempt to manipulate or influence the other person.

In addition, there may be individual differences in how people perceive and respond to non-verbal mirroring, regardless of cultural background. Some people may find it helpful and supportive, while others may feel uncomfortable or resistant – just consider childhood taunts and one child asking another to stop copying them after repeated phrases or body mimicry.

Therefore, when using non-verbal mirroring in coaching, it is important for coaches to be mindful of the cultural context and individual preferences of their clients, and to use mirroring techniques in a way that is appropriate and respectful. Coaches should also be prepared to adjust their approach based on feedback from the client and to be open to exploring alternative communication strategies if needed.

Verbal communication

In addition to considering the use of direct and indirect language, there are other points to think about while communicating. Metaphors and imagery are potentially very useful in communications because they make abstract ideas more tangible, and can wrap large amounts of subtle and detailed information, into a small package. Further to the use of metaphors is the use of clean language. Psychologist David Grove used this term to describe a questioning technique where the coach encouraged the coachee to form their own personal metaphors (Rees, 2009). Clean language involves using a set of precise and non-leading questions to guide a person's exploration of their thoughts, feelings and experiences. The questions are designed to keep the coach's influence to a minimum and to allow the person to delve deeper into their own mental landscape. Rees (2009) explains that clean language is a questioning and discussion technique used especially for discovering, exploring and working with people's own personal metaphors, and that coaches should listen attentively and ask simple questions to develop the conversation, clarify thoughts and explore the coachee's intentions.

The dialogue also needs to be considered. Dialogue is the to and fro of the conversation between the coach and the coachee. The coach needs to ensure they are allowing the coachee sufficient time to explore their thoughts and feelings, while also considering when it may be best to pose another question. The coach could think of the conversation like a Harkness aerial table map. A Harkness table is a specifically designed oval-style table to encourage contribution, collaboration and compassion in class discussions, and the tables were first used after American philanthropist Edward Harkness donated a large sum of money to an American high school in 1930. The table map is a drawing of a conversation with lines showing how the conservation flowed from one person to the next, to illustrate whether a good group discussion has occurred in terms of engagement.

According to Pearson (2016), the coach needs to adopt transactional analysis (TA) language where the language is from adult to adult, rather than from parent to child. The coach needs to be careful not to ask leading questions or steer the coachee in a particular direction. TA helps coaches and clients communicate better by recognising different talking styles (such as parent, adult, child). It improves conversations, resolves issues and boosts confidence. TA guides clients in setting goals, solving problems and expressing feelings honestly. Coaches use TA to create comfort and understanding.

In addition to considering the flow of the conversation, the coach needs to consider the push or challenge, and the pull or support. A coach may challenge through being more direct, or may use powerful questions where they send the client *'not to a specific destination, but in a direction filled with possible discoveries and mysteries ... to look inside or into the future. A powerful question is expansive and opens up further vistas for the client'* (Kimsey-House et al, 2011, p 70).

Active listening

Nigel Risner (2006) is an informative and hilarious motivational speaker. One memorable phrase from his talks was to 'be in the room' and give a task your full concentration; if you are listening to someone, you should be *actively* listening.

The listening element of a conversation is a coaching skill of value, as are the dialogue and questioning techniques used. Kimsey-House et al (2011) describe two aspects of listening, the first of which is awareness. This is described as being the information we draw in from all of our senses, and it includes non-verbal cues in addition to intuition, helping coaches reflect on the conversation by sensing what is inferred from a coachee's tone, volume, pace and even their pauses. Listening is also described in levels from 'internal listening' to 'focused' or more active listening, where the conversation includes *'you (the coach), the client, and an environment of information ... everything you can observe with your senses: what you see, hear, smell and feel-the tactile as well as the emotional senses'* (Kimsey-House et al, 2011, p 37).

Dan O'Connor (2011) explains that one of the key factors in being an active listener is considering your body language. He uses the acronym, ONE, where O stands for open body position, N stands for nodding to display empathy, and E stands for eye contact. However, O'Connor also explains that it is important to look away every ten seconds or so to avoid creeping out the other person.

Jim Knight (2007), author and researcher on instructional coaching, describes different listening strategies. An interesting recommendation he makes is to practise your own listening skills by talking with someone you think is a terrible listener.

Taberner and Taberner Siggins (2015) discuss how people have five listening choices. Listening is also sometimes described as having different levels of listening. The first listening choice is to ignore the speaker; the second is judgemental, and has a 'focus on me'; the third is a 'focus on you', which is judging the speaker in the coach's own context; the fourth choice is to 'focus on understanding' and be receptive, an active listener, non-judgemental and curious; and the fifth choice is 'focus on us':

> *Focus on us is about actively listening and remaining invested in the outcome of the conversation. We want to understand the perspectives of others and work together.*
> (Taberner and Taberner Siggins, 2015, p 47)

The power of curiosity

A coach needs to be authentic, because when you are *'not playing the role of professional coach, you create more relationship and more trust and clients will swing out more in their own lives'* (Kimsey-House et al, 2011, p 79). A coach who is authentic will be curious and use this skill to help the coachee. Taberner and Taberner Siggins (2015) discuss communication in *The Power of Curiosity*. They describe curiosity skills as being present to ABSORB the person's message, choosing how to listen and asking curious, open questions. They say:

> *You are present, aware of only what is going on right now. Being present helps us to find a place of calm where we feel grounded ... it's the only way we can access curiosity and intentionally listen to someone who is speaking to us.*
> (Taberner and Taberner Siggins, 2015, p 23)

Their acronym ABSORB stands for Attention; Body language and tone of voice; Stop and focus; Open to understanding not judging; Repeating through a paraphrase; and 'Becalm of the gremlins', or being aware of inner voices.

Coaching requires sensitivity and empathy, understanding each person's unique experiences and perspectives. Rogers (2017) comments on the importance of being aware of personality types including introvert and extrovert, and the effect of differences on the coach and coachee relationship. Effective coaching hinges on active listening skills, where coaches attentively grasp clients' concerns and goals; it also requires fostering open and respectful conversations, allowing clients to express themselves by freely and facilitating constructive dialogue. It is essential that the coach embraces individual differences and honours diverse backgrounds and values while tailoring their approach. Coaching is a collaborative journey that thrives on empathetic communication, active listening and a profound respect for each person's uniqueness.

STAFF TRAINING DISCUSSIONS

- What is the most important skill required by a good coach?
- How could a coach try to build trust within a coaching relationship?
- What clues might a coach notice about the coachee if they are listening with all their senses?
- What cultural differences might you need to consider with the individuals in your own organisation?

COACHING 'BOOK CLUB' SUGGESTIONS

The Power of Curiosity: How to Have Real Conversations That Create Collaboration, Innovation and Understanding by Kathy Taberner and Kirsten Siggins. I would recommend this book to read more about listening choices. When you understand them more, you will begin notice what listening choices you are making.

The Impact Code: Live the Life You Deserve by Nigel Risner. I would probably recommend listening to Risner speak over reading the book, as he is very funny, but his book does cover different personality types of monkey, elephant, dolphin and lion, and is useful to consider when coaching different personalities.

A FINAL NOTE ON TEACHER COACHING

TEACHER coaching questions

Coaching is about having a good conversation to help a coachee achieve their goal. The TEACHER model is designed to support a conversation, particularly for staff appraisals. A good conversation is open and authentic, and we should practise the required skills. We need to be able to listen actively; consider bias and perspectives and be non-judgemental; engage but not dominate; consider pauses and pace; express ourselves clearly and consider language that might appeal to the coachee; demonstrate empathy; consider tone and non-verbal cues; engage the suitable levels of push and pull on topics; and be able to end a conversation suitably. There is so much to consider that it is almost surprising that we are able to converse at all, but the good news is that we can improve each time we have a conversation. A conversation is not reading out a list of questions. Even though the TEACHER model helps provide a framework for a conversation, the order does not need to be rigidly adhered to. Many of the questions would also fit under multiple headings. Many of the questions can also be reversed, too – most of the those listed here have a positive vibe. Remember that a good conversation flows. Consider using the following list wisely!

Target questions

- Where would you like to meet?
- How have you been?
- Are you happy in knowing what information might be shared, and with whom?

- What has made you happy recently?
- What has been enjoyable about school life?
- What have been your highlights of the term?
- What do you see as the main parts of your job?
- What is the school vision?
- What goal would you like to focus on for today's session?
- What do you not want me to ask you about?
- What would you like to talk about the most?
- How does that help you?
- What would be the best use of our time today?
- What would an inspiring future look like for you?
- What would you like your legacy to be?
- If there was an outcome you were secretly hoping for, what would it be?
- Is there something in your work life that you would like to change?
- What are the main objectives of the school this year?
- What can you do to help the school be more successful?
- Are you happy with your work–life balance?
- What are the best things about school?
- How would you describe your attitude to learning?
- What behaviours are helping you at work?
- What do you think your goals might be?
- What are your current professional goals?
- How do you think achieving your goals will benefit your career?
- Why are you hoping to achieve these goals?
- What do you really want?
- Which goal will make you happiest?
- What is your *ikigai*?
- What is your BHAG?

Enlightenment questions

- Do you think you are a good role model? What makes a good role model?
- How would you describe your relationships at work?
- What could you do differently?

- Tell me about your use of feedback.
- Do you think you use assessments and data effectively?
- Do you think you prepare good resources?
- Describe your rapport with your pupils.
- Tell me about your classroom-management and time-management skills.
- What do you think about your own subject knowledge?
- Is there anything you could do better when communicating with parents?
- How do you encourage your pupils to be independent?
- What do you do to foster curiosity in your students?
- Do you think you are able to differentiate work effectively?
- Do you set high expectations for yourself and for others?
- What is required of you?
- Where in your body do you feel stuck?
- Are you aware of safeguarding requirements?
- What are your current issues?
- How do you cater for special education needs and disabilities (SEND) pupils?
- Do your lessons support the fundamental British values?
- Do you have a good understanding of school policies?
- How do you contribute to the wider life and ethos of your school?
- Are you aware of any new curriculum changes?
- Do you give yourself and your pupils time to reflect? What do you think might be behind that?
- What holds you back?
- What does your gremlin say?
- How open would you say you are to feedback?
- Is it okay if I give you some feedback?
- What went well during your lesson observation?
- What could have gone better during your lesson observation?
- What did you learn after reflecting on the lesson you taught?
- What made the lesson great in the best lesson you taught this year?
- What did you learn from being observed or watching a video of your teaching?

- Where are you currently positioned on Maslow's hierarchy of needs?
- Describe your 'wheel of life'. How does this make you feel?
- What are the challenges you face?
- What is happening right now?
- Who says that? How do you know?
- If you spoke to others about your goals, what would they say?
- How far have you come since our last meeting?
- What advice would you give to someone else about that?
- How does this align with your core values?

Achievement questions

- What have you already accomplished?
- What is your biggest accomplishment in your teaching career?
- What have you done that had the greatest positive impact on a pupil?
- What have you done that had the greatest positive impact on another member of staff?
- What courses or training have you done recently?
- When have you performed most productively?
- What have you achieved recently that made you happy?
- What are you most proud of?
- What is your biggest failure that you can celebrate because it helped you learn?
- What is working well right now?
- What do you get complimented on the most?
- What are your biggest achievements this term?
- How do you note your achievements?
- Who have you shared your success with? How will you celebrate that?

Choice questions

- Have you been in a similar situation before? What helped?
- What would happen if you did nothing?
- What is the best thing about this option?

- What is the biggest change you are willing to make?
- What are you afraid of?
- What would you gain by doing that?
- What are some of your options?
- What are five other ways you could achieve your goal?
- If time and money were not an issue, what would you do?
- What are the obstacles to you achieving your goals?
- What would you do if the obstacles were removed?
- What have you seen others do that might work for you?
- What is holding you back?
- Which option grabs you? Which choice do you like best?
- Which goals do you choose to set?

Help questions

- What is your specific goal?
- Did I hear you say that …?
- How can you make your goal measurable so it is obvious when it has been achieved?
- Do you think your goal is achievable?
- What makes this goal relevant?
- When will you have completed your goal by?
- On a scale of 1 to 10, how likely are you to achieve your goal in the time set?
- How can we improve that score?
- How can you achieve your goals and maintain a healthy work–life balance?
- What options are you going to action?
- How are you recording you goals and your plan?
- Would splitting your goals into smaller steps be helpful? How are you going to do that?
- What are your biggest priorities?
- If you were 'at your best', what would you do right now?
- Are there any resources you need?
- How can leaders help you?
- Is there anyone who can help you?

- What will your first step be?
- What are the skills you need to achieve your goal?
- How will you know you are making progress?

Encouragement questions

- Can you visualise your goal?
- What will your first small win be? How will you celebrate?
- What will it feel like when you have achieved your goal?
- What is motivating you towards your goal?
- When are you going to take your first step?
- Do you feel you should already have achieved your goal? What is slowing you down?
- What steps have you already taken?
- How can I help?
- What is keeping you going?
- What are two things you could do next week?
- Imagine you have just had a great week. What did you do?
- What are you going to do immediately after this session?
- What would make this more enjoyable?
- Who can support you?
- How amazing does it feel to have a small win already?

Reflection questions

- What are your main take-aways from today?
- Is there anything else you want to cover that you have not been able to share today?
- What was your biggest win today?
- How will you evaluate the success of coaching?
- What is the best bit about being coached?
- What have you learned about yourself?
- Have you been happier since you started coaching?
- Was your goal in alignment with your school's goals?
- What are your new goals?

- Now that you have achieved your goals, is there anything you would do differently next time?
- How do you feel now you have achieved your goal?
- When you achieve your goal, how important will the journey have been?

Phew!

Phew! You've made it to the end. You are now invited to reflect on the journey through the world of coaching, from its inception and evolution to its practical implementation. This journey has illuminated the essence of coaching, the transformative power it holds, and the diverse models that have shaped its development over the years. As we stand at the crossroads of understanding coaching's profound impact on individuals, teams and organisations, we are reminded that coaching is more than a technique; it is a mindset, a culture and a way of being.

By embracing the TEACHER Coaching model of Target, Enlightenment, Achievement, Choice, Help, Encouragement and Reflection, and the principles of building a coaching culture, you are embarking on a path of continuous growth, collaboration and learning. As both coach and coachee, you can grasp the significance of empathy, curiosity and effective communication. With each chapter of this book, you have delved deeper into the heart of coaching, recognising its potential to shape not only individual lives, but also entire educational institutions.

Equipped with insights, knowledge and practical strategies, you are prepped for a new era where coaching transforms not only how you work and learn, but how you thrive as human beings striving for enlightenment, happiness and success.

Good luck on your coaching journey!

REFERENCES

Achor, S (2011) *The Happiness Advantage*. London: Virgin Books.

Action Learning Associates (2023) Home page. [online] Available at: www.actionlearningassociates.co.uk (accessed 25 October 2023).

Amabile, T and Kramer, S (2011) *The Progress Principle: Using Small Wins to Ignite Joy*. Cambridge, MA: Harvard Business School.

Anderson, C, Frankovelgia, C and Hernez-Broome, G (2016) *Creating Coaching Culture: What Business Leaders Expect and Strategies to Get There*. [online] Available at: https://cclinnovation.org/wp-content/uploads/2016/02/creatingcoachingcultures.pdf (accessed 11 August 2023).

Appleby, J (2022) *Identifying and Coaching Different Personality Types*. New York: Business Expert Press.

Bakhshi, H, Downing, J A, Osborne, M A and Schneider, P (2017) *The Future of Skills: Employment in 2030*. London: Pearson and Nesta.

Bansal, P and Tripathi, P C (2017) A Literature Review on Training Needs Analysis. *International Journal of Engineering Technology Science and Research*, 119(1): 50–6.

Berger, J (2013) *Contagious: How to Build Word of Mouth in the Digital Age*. London: Simon and Schuster.

Bernstein, G (2019) *Super Attractor*. New York: Hay House.

Brehm, S S and Brehm, J W (2013) *Psychological Reactance: A Theory of Freedom and Control*. Cambridge, MA: Academic Press.

Brinkerhoff, R O (2018) *The Success Case Method: Find Out Quickly What's Working and What's Not*. Oakland, CA: Berrett-Koehler.

Bryson, A, Forth, J and Stokes, L (2014) *Does Worker Well-being Affect Workplace Performance? Evidence from Small Enterprises*. [online]

Available at: https://assets.publishing.service.gov.uk/government/uploads/system/uploads/attachment_data/file/366637/bis-14-1120-does-worker-wellbeing-affect-workplace-performance-final.pdf (accessed 25 August 2023).

Burns, J M (2010) *Leadership.* New York: HarperCollins.

Businessballs (2021) Kirkpatrick's Evaluation Method. [online] Available at: www.businessballs.com/hr-training/kirkpatrick-evaluation-model (accessed 25 August 2023).

Carnegie, D (2023) *How to Win Friends and Influence People.* New York: Bibliotheka.

Carter, W, Channon, J and Kane, L (2018) Evaluation of Coaching in the National Health Service: A Mixed Methods Study. *International Journal of Evidence-Based Coaching and Mentoring*, 16(2): 104–18.

Chapman, B (2013) Outsourcing: Don't Default to Cost Reduction but to Getting the Most Out of Your People. *The Guardian*, 18 January. [online] Available at: www.theguardian.com/small-business-network/2013/jan/18/outsourcing-dont-default-cost-reduction (accessed 25 August 2023).

Chapman, B (2016) *Everybody Matters: The Extraordinary Power of Caring for Your People Like Family.* Harmondsworth: Penguin.

Chartered Management Institute (2018) *The Business Benefits of Management and Leadership Development.* London: CMI.

Clear, J (2018) *Atomic Habits.* New York: Avery.

Coach 4 Growth (2022) ACHIEVE coaching model. [online] Available at: https://coach4growth.com/achieve-coaching-model (accessed 25 August 2023).

Collins, J (2001) *Good to Great.* New York: Century.

Collins, J C and Porras, J I (2004) *Built to Last: Successful Habits of Visionary Companies.* London: Random House.

Cook, C and Artino, J (2016) A Motivation to Learn: An Overview of Contemporary Theories. *Medical Education*, 50(1): 983–1077.

Covey, S R (2004) *The 7 Habits of Highly Effective People: Restoring the Character Ethic.* New York: Free Press.

Covey, S (2004) *The 7 Habits of Highly Effective People - Powerful Lessons in Personal Change.* London: Simon and Schuster UK Ltd.

Crane, T (2012) *The Heart of Coaching.* Los Angeles: FTA Press.

Csíkszentmihályi, M (2001) *Flow: The Psychology of Optimal Experience.* London: Harper Collins.

Damkier, S and Ozer, S (2022) *Social Identity and Well-being: A Cross-Cultural Examination of Social Identity and Well-being in Light of the Accelerating Cultural Globalisation.* [online] Available at: https://journals.sagepub.com/doi/full/10.1177/09713336221080640 (accessed 23 November 2023).

Day, E (2019) *How To Fail: Everything I've Ever Learned from Things Going Wrong.* London: 4th Estate.

de Bono, E (1985) *Six Thinking Hats.* New York: Little, Brown and Company.

Dominican University (2015) *Goals Research Summary.* [online] Available at: www.dominican.edu/academics/ahss/undergraduate-programs/psych/faculty/assets-gail-matthews/researchsummary2.pdf (accessed 22 October 2023).

Dorrance Hall, E (2019) Why We Hate People Telling Us What to Do. *Psychology Today,* 6 June. [online] Available at: www.psychologytoday.com/gb/blog/conscious-communication/201906/why-we-hate-people-telling-us-what-do?scrlybrkr=6a569968 (accessed 25 August 2023).

Downey, M (2002) *A Guide to Coaching and Being Coached.* Maidenhead: Open University Press.

Drucker, P (1954) *The Practice of Management.* New York: Harper & Row.

Dweck, C S (2013) *Mindset: Changing The Way You Think to Fulfil Your Potential.* London: Constable & Robinson.

Eldridge, F and Dembkowski, S (2004) Beyond GROW: A New Coaching Model. *The International Journal of Mentoring and Coaching*, 1(1). [online] Available at: www.coachingnetwork.org.uk/information-portal/Articles/pdfs/CtC3.pdf (accessed 22 October 2023).

Eleisha Training (2014) Trust: Thirteen Trust Building Behaviours of Leaders. Available at: www.eleishatraining.com/trust-thirteen-trust-building-behaviors-of-leaders (accessed 22 October 2023).

EMCC Global (2020) *EMCC Global Code of Ethics*. [online] Available at: https://emccuk.org/Common/Uploaded%20files/Policies/Global_Code_of_Ethics_EN_v3.pdf (Accessed 25 August 2023).

Ennis, S and Otto, J (2015) *The Executive Coaching Handbook: Principles and Guidelines for a Successful Coaching Partnership* (6th ed). [online] Available at: https://theexecutivecoachingforum.com/docs/default-document-library/tecf-6th-ed.pdf (accessed 25 August 2023).

Favell, I (2016) Coaching, Performance Management and Reflecting on Reflections. *International Journal of Mentoring and Coaching in Education*, 5(3): 173–85.

Funck, F (2023) How to Instill a Coaching Culture. [online] Available at: https://ccl2020stg.ccl.org/articles/leading-effectively-articles/instill-coaching-culture (accessed 15 August 2023).

Gallwey, W T (1974) *The Inner Game of Tennis*. New York: Random House.

Gallwey, W T (2000) *The Inner Game of Work*. New York: Random House.

Germain, J (2008) Why a Senior Manager Needs a Mentor. *Journal of Business Strategy*, 29(5): 45–50.

Gilbert, A and Whittleworth, K (2009) *Oscar Coaching Model: Helping Managers to Improve Performance and Professional Effectiveness*. London: Worth Consulting.

Girling, N (2021) Coaching or Mentoring: What's the Difference? [online] Available at: www.managers.org.uk/knowledge-and-insights/blog/coaching-or-mentoring-whats-the-difference/ (accessed 21 November 2023).

Goleman, D (2020) *Emotional Intelligence: Why It Can Matter More Than IQ.* London: Bloomsbury.

Grant, A (2016) *Originals: How Non-Conformists Change the World.* London: WH Allen.

Grint, K (2010) Wicked Problems and Clumsy Solutions: The Role of Leadership. In Brookes, S and Grint, K (eds), *The New Public Leadership Challenge.* London: Palgrave Macmillan.

Hall, E T (1976) *Beyond Culture*, New York: Doubleday.

Hawkins, P (2012) *Creating a Coaching Culture: Developing a Coaching Strategy for Your Organization.* Maidenhead: Open University Press.

Hicks, B, Carter, A and Sinclair A (2013) *Impact of Coaching on Employee Well-being, Engagement and Job Satisfaction.* [online] Available at: www.employment-studies.co.uk/system/files/resources/files/hrp8.pdf (accessed 25 August 2023).

Hill, E (2019) How to Give Feedback Constructively. [online] Available at: www.forbes.com/sites/forbescoachescouncil/2019/05/20/how-to-give-feedback-constructively/?sh=5ff5d9cb5f08 (accessed 7 May 2023).

Hirsh, W (2009) Clarifying Your Learning and Development Strategy. *Strategic HR Review*, 8(4): 17–22. https://doi.org/10.1108/14754390910956387.

Hofstede, G (2010) *Cultures and Organizations: Software of the Mind* (3rd ed). New York: McGraw-Hill.

Hollweck (2019) I Love This Stuff – A Canadian Case Study of Mentor Coach Well-Being. [online] Available at: www.researchgate.net/publication/335659645_I_love_this_stuff_a_Canadian_case_study_of_mentor-coach_well-being (accessed 19 November 2023).

Horowitz, B (2014) *The Hard Thing About Hard Things: Building a Business When There are No Easy Answers.* New York: HarperCollins.

Hudson Institute (2018) A Coaching Culture Matters and Here's Why. [online] Available at: https://hudsoninstitute.com/a-coaching-culture-matters (accessed 25 August 2023).

International Coaching Federation (2021) *ICF Code of Ethics*. [online] Available at: https://hudsoninstitute.com/a-coaching-culture-matters (accessed 25 August 2023).

Kimsey-House, H, Kimsey-House, K, Sandahl, P and Whitworth, L (2011) *Co-active Coaching: Changing Business, Transforming Lives*. London: Nicholas Brealey.

Kishimi, I and Koga, F (2017) *The Courage to Be Disliked: How to Free Yourself, Change Your Life and Achieve Real Happiness*. London: Allen & Unwin.

Knight, J (2007) *Instructional Coaching: A Partnership Approach to Improving Instruction*. Thousand Oaks, CA: Corwin Press.

Knight, R (2015) How to Run a Meeting of People from Different Cultures. *Harvard Business Review*, 4 December. [online] Available at: https://hbr.org/2015/12/how-to-run-a-meeting-of-people-from-different-cultures (accessed 7 October 2023).

Koch, R (2004) *Living the 80/20 Way: Work Less, Worry Less, Succeed More, Enjoy More*. London: Nicholas Brealey.

Kotler, S (2014) *The Rise of Superman: Decoding the Science of Ultimate Human Performance*. Sacramento, CA: New Harvest.

Kotter, J (2012) *Leading Change* Boston: Harvard Business Review Press.

Kraft, M A, Blazar, D and Hogan, D (2018) The Effect of Teacher Coaching on Instruction and Achievement: A Meta Analysis of the Causal Evidence. [online] Available at https://scholar.harvard.edu/files/mkraft/files/kraft_blazar_hogan_2018_teacher_coaching.pdf (accessed 20 November 2023).

Kram, K E (1983) Phases of the Mentor Relationship. *Academy of Management Journal*, 26(4): 608–25.

Kübler-Ross, E (1969) *On Death & Dying*. New York: Simon & Schuster/Touchstone.

Lee, M (2014) Transformational Leadership: Is It Time for a Recall? *International Journal of Management and Applied Research*, 1(1): 17–29.

Lee, Y-C, Lin, Y-C, Huang, C-H and Fredrickson, B L (2013) The Construct and Measurement of Peace of Mind. *Journal of Happiness Studies*, 14: 571–90.

Leonard, T J (1998) *The Portable Coach: 28 Sure-fire Strategies for Business and Personal Success.* New York: Simon and Schuster.

Lewin, K, Lippitt, R and White, R K (1939) Patterns of Aggressive Behavior in Experimentally Created 'Social Climates'. *Journal of Social Psychology*, 10: 271–99.

Locke, E A and Latham, G P (1990) *A Theory of Goal Setting & Task Performance.* Englewood Cliffs, NJ: Prentice-Hall.

Lopez-Garrido, G (2023) Self Determination Theory: How It Explains Motivation. *Simply Psychology*, 10 July. [online] Available at: www.simplypsychology.org/self-determination-theory.html (accessed 28 October 2023).

Lu, H-L (2010) Research on Peer Coaching in Preservice Teacher Education – A Review of Literature. [online] Available at: www.researchgate.net/publication/248526944_Research_on_peer_coaching_in_preservice_teacher_education_-_A_review_of_literature (accessed 21 November 2023).

Luhmann, M (2017) The Development of Subjective Well-being. [online] Available at: www.researchgate.net/publication/292604434_Development_of_Subjective_Well-Being (Accessed 25 August 2023).

Lundy, O and Cowling, A (1996) *Strategic Human Resource Management.* London: Routledge.

MacLennan, B (2017). *Coaching and Mentoring.* London: Routledge.

MacLennan, S, Stead, I and Little, A (2019) *Wellbeing Guidance for Appraisal: Supplementary Green Book Guidance.* London: HM Treasury.

Maslow, A (1943) A Theory of Human Motivation. *Psychological Review*, 50: 370–96.

Marsick, V J and Neil, J (2005) The Many Faces of Action Learning. *Management Learning*, 30(2): 159–76.

Martinez-Lorente, A R (1998) Total Quality Management: Origins and Evolution of the Term. *The TQM Magazine*. [online] Available at: www.emerald.com/insight/content/doi/10.1108/09544789810231261/full/html (accessed 15 August 2023).

McBain, R, Ghobadian, A, Switzer, J, Wilton, P, Woodman, P and Pearson, G (2012) The Business Benefits of Management and Leadership Development: Executive Summary. [online] Available at: www.bl.uk/britishlibrary/~media/bl/global/business-and-management/pdfs/non-secure/b/u/s/business-benefits-of-management-and-leadership-development-summary-report.pdf (accessed 11 August 2023).

McKergow, M and Jackson, P Z (2002) *The Solutions Focus: Making Coaching and Change SIMPLE.* London: Nicholas Brealey.

McLeod, A (2003) *Performance Coaching: The Handbook for Managers, HR Professionals and Coaches.* London: Crown House.

Megginson, D and Clutterbuck, D (2005) *Techniques for Coaching and Mentoring.* London: Routledge.

Meister, C, Willyerd, K and Zemke, R (2010) Mentoring Millennials. *Harvard Business Review*, May. [online] Available at: https://hbr.org/2010/05/mentoring-millennials (accessed 25 August 2023).

Molinksy, A (2013) Giving Feedback Across Cultures. *Harvard Business Review*, 15 February. [online] Available at: https://hbr.org/2013/02/giving-feedback-across-cultures (accessed 25 October 2023).

Morrison McGill, R (2017) *Mark. Plan. Teach.* London: Bloomsbury.

Moen, F and Allgood, E (2009) Coaching and the Effect on Self-efficacy. *Journal of College Teaching and Learning*, 6(11): 47–54.

Mosston, M and Ashworth, S (1994) *Teaching Physical Education* (4th ed). New York: Macmillan.

van Nieuwerburgh, C, Barr, M, Munro, C, Noon, H and Arifin, D (2020) Experiences of Aspiring School Principals Receiving Coaching as Part of a Leadership Development Programme. [online] Available at: www.

researchgate.net/publication/341710631_Experiences_of_aspiring_school_principals_receiving_coaching_as_part_of_a_leadership_development_programme (accessed 21 November 2023).

O'Connor, D (2011) *Say This – NOT THAT! Power Phrases Designed to Help You Communicate with More Power, Tact, and Finesse, Along with Danger Phrases to Avoid at All Costs.* New York: Power Diversity.

OECD (2012) *Teaching in Focus.* [online] Available at: www.oecd.org/education/talis/teachinginfocus.htm (accessed 15 August 2023).

Oettingen, G (2014) WOOP My Life. [online] Available at https://woopmylife.org/en/home (accessed 4 December 2023).

Oppland, M (2016) 8 Traits of Flow According to Mihaly Csikszentmihalyi. [online] Available at: https://positivepsychology.com/mihaly-csikszentmihalyi-father-of-flow (accessed 15 August 2023).

Oswald, A, Proto, E and Sgroi, D (2015) *Happiness and Productivity.* [online] Available at: https://wrap.warwick.ac.uk/63228/7/WRAP_Oswald_681096.pdf (accessed 25 August 2023).

Panagiotis, M, Sahinidis, A and Polychronopoulos, G (2015) Organizational Culture and Motivation in the Public Sector: The Case of the City of Zografou. *Procedia Economics and Finance*, 14: 415–24.

Parsloe, E and Wray, M (2000) Coaching and Mentoring: Practical Methods to Improve Learning. *Work Study*, 49(6). https://doi.org/10.1108/ws.2000.07949fae.002.

Pascale, R and Sternin, J (2005) Your Company's Secret Change Agents. [online] Available at: https://hbr.org/2005/05/your-companys-secret-change-agents (accessed 25 August 2023).

Passmore, J (2007) An Integrative Model for Executive Coaching. [online] Available at: www.researchgate.net/publication/232596843_An_Integrative_Model_for_Executive_Coaching (accessed 25 August 2023).

Pearson, P (2016) Coaching or Mentoring. *The Journal of Values-Based Leadership,* 9(1): 1–12.

References

Pedler, M (2016) Revans, Reginald: The Pioneer of Action Learning. In Szabla, D B (ed), *The Palgrave Handbook of Organizational Change Thinkers*. [online] Available at: https://link.springer.com/referenceworkentry/10.1007/978-3-319-49820-1_20-2 (Accessed 25 August 2023).

Pedler, M, Burgoyne, J G and Boydell, T (1997) *The Learning Company*. New York: McGraw-Hill.

Pegg, M (1999) The Art of Mentoring. *Industrial and Commercial Training*, 31(4): 136–41.

Phillips-Jones, L (2003) *75 Things to Do with Your Mentee: Practical Ideas for Mentoring*. Oxford: Blackwell.

Poutanen, E (2018) Understand Your Social Brain: The SCARF Model. [online] Available at: https://neuroleadership.fi/blog/understand-your-social-brain-the-scarf-model (accessed 25 August 2023).

Prochaska, J O and DiClemente, C C (1983) Stages and Processes of Self-change of Smoking: Toward an Integrative Model of Change. *Journal of Consulting and Clinical Psychology*, 51(3): 390–5.

Prosci (2023) ADKAR model. [online] Available at: www.prosci.com/adkar/adkar-model (accessed 25 August 2023).

Ragins, B R and Cotton, J (1999) Mentor Functions and Outcomes: A Comparison of Men and Women in Formal and Informal Mentoring Relationships. *Journal of Applied Psychology*, 84(4): 529–50.

Rees, J (2009) Clean Language: David Grove Questioning Method. [online] Available at: www.businessballs.com/communication-skills/clean-language-david-grove-questioning-method (accessed 25 August 2023).

Rees, J (2017) *Built for Greatness: Inspirational Quotes and Lessons from the Great*. Self-published.

Renton, J (2009) *Coaching and Mentoring: What They Are and How to Make the Most of Them*. London: Chartered Institute of Personnel and Development.

Richardson, A (1967) Mental Practice: A Review and Discussion (Part II). *Research Quarterly*, 38: 263–73.

Ries, A and Trout, J (2001) *Positioning: The Battle for Your Mind*. New York: McGraw-Hill.

Risner, N (2006) *The Impact Code: Live the Life You Deserve*. Chichester: Capstone.

Ritt, M J (2002) *Napoleon Hill's Keys to Positive Thinking*. London: Judy Piatkus.

Robertson, I and Cooper, C (2011) *Well-being: Productivity and Happiness at Work*. New York: Springer.

Rogers, L (2017) *Coaching with Personality Type*. London: Nicholas Brealey.

Sanborn, M (2005) *The Fred Factor*. New York: Random House.

Sanchez-Burks, J, Blount, C A and Bartel, S (2009) Performance in Intercultural Interactions at Work: Cross-cultural Differences in Response to Behavioral Mirroring. *Journal of Applied Psychology*, 94(1): 216–23.

Sandahl, J (2020) The Business Case for Team Coaching. [online] Available at: https://teamcoachinginternational.com/business-case-team-coaching (accessed 25 August 2023).

Schilder, D (2015) The Hersey-Blanchard Situational Leadership Theory: Choosing the Right Leadership Style for the Right People. [online] Available at: www.donnaschilder.com/wp-content/uploads/2015/09/The-Hersey-Blanchard-Situational-Leadership%C2%AE-Theory.pdf (accessed 25 August 2023).

Schön, D (1983) *The Reflective Practitioner: How Professionals Think in Action*. New York: Basic Books.

Schwartz, S H (2012) An Overview of the Schwartz Theory of Basic Values. [online] Available at: https://scholarworks.gvsu.edu/orpc/vol2/iss1/11 (accessed 25 August 2023).

Senge, P M (1997) *The Fifth Discipline: The Art and Practice of the Learning Organization.* London: Century Business.

Senge, P M (2007) *Schools That Learn: A Fifth Discipline Fieldbook for Educators, Parents, and Everyone Who Cares About Education.* London: Nicholas Brealey.

Serrat, O (2017) *Knowledge Solutions: Tools, Methods, and Approaches to Drive Organizational Performance.* Singapore: Springer.

Sketch, E, Flick, A and Israel, G D (2001) *Mentoring and Coaching Help Employees Grow.* Miami: University of Florida. [online] Available at: https://edis.ifas.ufl.edu/pdffiles/hr/hr02200.pdf (accessed 24 October 2023).

Smale, C (2014) *A–Z Coaching Handbook.* London: Smale.

Sparrow, S (2007) Performance Improvement Coaching Models. [online] Available at: www.personneltoday.com/hr/performance-improvement-coaching-models-the-real-deal (accessed 25 August 2023).

Studer, B, Geniole, S N, Becker, M L, Eisenegger, C and Knecht, S (2016) Inducing Illusory Control Ensures Persistence When Rewards Fade and When Others Outperform Us. [online] Available at: www.researchgate.net/publication/341474592_Inducing_illusory_control_ensures_persistence_when_rewards_fade_and_when_others_outperform_us (accessed 25 August 2023).

Sustainable Developments Solutions Network (2023) World Happiness Report. [online] Available at: https://worldhappiness.report/ed/2023/ (accessed 21 November 2023).

Syed, M (2016) *Black Box Thinking: Marginal Gains and the Secrets of High Performance.* London: John Murray.

Syed, M (2019) *Rebel Ideas.* London: John Murray.

Taberner, K and Taberner Siggins, K (2015) *The Power of Curiosity: How to Have Real Conversations That Create Collaboration, Innovation and Understanding.* New York: Morgan James.

Tahir, M (2019) Lewin's Force Field Analysis (Change Management). [online] Available at: https://changemanagementinsight.com/lewins-force-field-analysis-change-management (accessed 15 August 2023).

Tannenbaum, R and Schmidt, W (1958) How to Choose a Leadership Pattern. *Harvard Business Review*, 36(2): 95–101.

Taylor, D (2011) Wellbeing and Welfare: A Psychosocial Analysis of Being Well and Doing Well Enough. In Lovell, T and Richards, B (eds), *Improving Health and Wellbeing: How Can Evidence-Based Practice Contribute?* Chichester: Wiley-Blackwell.

Tieger, P D, Barron, B and Tieger, K (2007) *Do What You Are*. New York: Little Brown.

Tuckman, B (1965) Developmental Sequence in Small Groups. *Psychological Bulletin*, 63(6): 384–99.

Veitze, J, Juang, L, and Schachner, M (2019) Peer cultural socialisation: A Resource for Minority Students' Cultural Identity, Life Satisfaction, and School Values. [online] Available at: www.tandfonline.com/doi/full/10.1080/14675986.2019.1586213 (accessed 23 November 2023).

Warr, P, Bird, M and Rackham, N (1970) *Evaluation of Management Training*. London: Gower Press.

Whitmore, J (2002) *Coaching for Performance*. London: Nicholas Brealey.

Willis, J (2007) The Neuroscience of Joyful Education. [online] Available at: www.ascd.org/el/articles/the-neuroscience-of-joyful-education (accessed 25 August 2023).

Worton, S and Ippolito, K (2014) *A Practical Guide to Giving Effective Feedback*. London: Imperial College, University of London.

Zenger, J and Stinnett, K (2010) *The Extraordinary Coach: How the Best Leaders Help Others Grow*. New York: McGraw-Hill.

INDEX

ABSORB, 144

ACHIEVE model, 31–2, 85

Achievement stage (TEACHER model), 80–4
    celebrations in, 83–4
    recording in, 83
    types and strengths, 82–3

action learning, 53–6

active listening, 32, 109, 136, 137, 139, 142–3, 144

ADDIE model, 89, 91

ADKAR change model, 113, 114, 115

AID model, 73

Anderson Value of Learning model, 117

ASK ABE model, 72

'At My Best' cards, 83

Atomic Habits (Clear), 90

A–Z Coaching Handbook (Smale), 111

BHAGs (Big Hairy Audacious Goals), 87, 88

Black Box Thinking (Syed), 44

Built to Last (Collins and Porras), 39

Cartesian questions, 85

CEDAR feedback, 73

change, adoption to
    in climate, 113
    collaboration, 113–14
    communication, 114–15
    embed, 115
    goals, 115

change curve model, 110

change model
    ADKAR, 113, 114, 115
    eight-step, 112
    Stages of Change model (or Transtheoretical model), 30, 33
    theory of, 120

Choice stage (TEACHER model)
    barriers or obstacles, 86
    goals, 84–5
    options in, 85
    priorities, 87–8

CLEAR model, 25–6, 27

clock-building, 39

coach and coachee relationship, 62

coach qualities, 126–7
   confidentiality, need for, 127
   sensitivity, need for, 126–7
Coach U model, 28–9
coaching
   in 1930s, 21–3
   in 1950s, 23
   in 1960s, 23–4
   in 1970s, 24–5
   in 1980s, 25–7
   in 1990s, 27–9
   in 2000s, 29–33
   in 2010s, 34–5
   in 2020s, 35–6
   appraisals, success of, 120–3
   in classrooms, need for, 7–10
   definitions of, 4–5
   meaning of, 1–3
   versus mentoring, 10–12
   origin of, 4
   process of, 5–7
   purpose of, 3–4
   teams, 49–52
Coaching and Mentoring (Renton), 19
coaching cards, 69
coaching conversations, 47, 62–3, 65
coaching culture, 40
   barriers, 110–12
   benefits of, 45–6
   change, adopting to, 112–16
   developing, 105–6
   embedding, 49
   and happiness, 46–7
   in school learning, 55–6
   leadership and vision, 107
   leadership coach skills, 109–10
   leadership styles, 108
   positioning, 106
Coaching for Performance (Whitmore), 19
coaching impact, measuring, 116–20
coaching leadership style, 108
coaching spectrum, 14–15
Co-active Coaching (Kimsey-House et al), 37
Co-active model, 27–8
code of ethics, 67, 127–9
command style, 2
Contagious (Berger), 122
Content, Input, Reaction, Outcome (CIRO) evaluating model, 115–16

context cultures, 136
contracting, 65–6
convergent teaching style, 2
Courage to be Disliked, The (Kishima and Koga), 96
culture
    differences, 129–31
    theory of, 135–8
curiosity, power of, 144

divergent teaching style, 2
diversity, 102

ELSA (Emotional Literacy Support Assistant), 17
Emotional Intelligence (EQ), 109
Emotional Intelligence (Goleman), 124
Encouragement stage (TEACHER model), 92–9
    extrinsic motivation, 92–3
    flow, 97–9
    intrinsic motivation and SDT, 95
    Maslow's hierarchy of needs, 95–7
    visualisation, 93–5
Enlightenment stage (TEACHER model), 71–80
    clarity, 79–80

    feedback, 72–7
    feedforward, 73
    perspective, 77–9
    self-assessment, 71–80
environment, 64–5
Eudaimonia, 48
European Mentoring and Coaching Council (EMCC), 127
Everybody Matters (Chapman), 109
evidence, 76
expectancy-value model, 93
expectations, 67–8
Extraordinary Coach, The (Zenger and Stinnett), 35

FAST feedback, 73
feedback, 72–7
    in coaching conversations, 138–9
    feedback sandwich, 75
    framing, 74–5
    models of, 73–4
    need for, 41–2
feedforward, 73
'Field of Dreams' (Robinson), 99
Fifth Discipline, The (Senge), 42, 57
5 Whys technique, 86

formal mentoring, 12–13
framing, 74–5
FRED (Find, Reward, Educate, Demonstrate), 92
FUEL coaching model, 34–5

gamification, 118
Gantt chart, 16, 89, 119
goal setting theory, 88
goals
    potential, 68
    purpose of, 69–70
Good to Great (Collins), 126
GROW model, 26–7, 29, 59–60
growth mindset, 43–5
Growth Mindset (Dweck), 43
guided discovery, 24

happier workforce, 48–9
Happiness Advantage, The (Achor), 57, 81
happiness in school, 48
Hard Thing about Hard Things, The (Horowitz), 109
Help stage (TEACHER model), 88–92
    Kaizen, 91
    marginal gains, 90
    plan, 89–90
    plan implementation, 91–2
    SMART and ADDIE, 89
Hofstede dimensions, 131–5
    individualism versus collectivism, 132
    indulgence versus restraint, 135
    long-term orientation versus short-term orientation, 134–5
    masculinity-femininity, 132–3
    power distance, 131–2
    uncertainty avoidance, 133–4
How to Win Friends and Influence People (Carnegie), 21, 38

idea generation, 101
Ikigai model, 69
Impact Code (Risner), 145
individualism versus collectivism, 132
indulgence versus restraint, 135
informal mentoring, 12–13
informative/constructive feedback, 75
inner game, 24–5
Inner Game of Tennis, The (Gallwey), 24
Inner Game of Work, The (Gallwey), 19

Instructional Coaching (Knight), 37
instructional coaching model, 33
intrinsic motivation and SDT, 95

Johari window, 76–7
Journal of Happiness Studies, 47

Kaizen, 91
Kaufman's model, 118
Kirkpatrick Model, 117–18

Leadership (Burns), 108
leadership barriers, 111
leadership behaviour continuum, 108
leadership coach skills, 109–10
Leading Change (Kotter), 124
learning organisation, 42–3
long-term orientation versus short-term orientation, 134–5

management by objectives (MBO), 23
marginal gains, 90
Mark. Plan. Teach (McGill), 57
masculinity-femininity, 132–3
Maslow's hierarchy of needs, 95–7

Mental Contrasting with Implementation Intentions (MCII), 32
mentoring, 10–12
mentoring, stages of, 67–8
Microsoft Excel, 89
Microsoft Forms, 70, 118
Microsoft Learn, 17
Microsoft Planner, 89
Mindset (Dweck), 57
mistakes, learning from, 102–3
modern classrooms, 8

non-verbal communication, 139–41

ONE, 143
open mindedness, 102
Organisation for Economic Co-operation and Development (OECD), 61–2
Originals (Grant), 104
OSCAR model, 29–30
OSKAR model, 29

Pareto Principle, 78
PDSA (plan-do-study-assess), 107
Peace of Mind Scale, 47
PEG model, 79
Pendleton feedback, 74

Performance Coaching, 87
Performance Coaching (McLeod), 104
Phillips Return on Investment Model, 118
Pip Decks, 85
pleasantries, 65
Portable Coach, The (Leonard), 29
Positioning: The Battle for Your Mind (Ries and Trout), 106
power distance, 131–2
Power of Curiosity, The (Taberner and Siggins), 144, 145
Practice of Management, The (Drucker), 23
pre-meeting, 62–3
Pre-Senior Baccalaureate (PSB), 7
Progress Principle, The (Amabile and Kramer), 82
pupil welfare, 47–8

real-world problem, types of, 54
Rebel Ideas, 78
Reflection stage (TEACHER model)
    appraisal, 103
    flexibility, 101–3
    reflection-on-action, 99–101
reflection-on-action, 99–101

Reginald Revans (Pedler), 54
respectful feedback, 74
Rethinking Positive Thinking (Oettingen), 32
return on investment (ROI), 119
Revan's model of action learning, 54
Revans' law, 54
RISE feedback, 74–6
    evidence, 76
    informative/constructive feedback, 75
    respectful feedback, 74
    specific feedback, 75–6
role-play, 78–9
root cause analysis (RCA), 86

SBI feedback, 73
scaling techniques, 29, 84
self-assessment, 71–80
self-determination theory (SDT), 95
7 Habits of Highly Effective People (Covey), 71, 104
Six Thinking Hats (De Bono), 77
SMART model, 17, 88, 89
Socratic method, 24
specific feedback, 75–6
Spectrum of Teaching Styles, 14, 24

Spectrum of Teaching Styles for Physical Education, The (Mosston), 1

Stages of Change model (or Transtheoretical model), 30, 33

star-shaped model, 28

STEPPPA (or STEPPA) model, 31

STEPPS, 122–3

Success Case Method (Brinkerhoff), 118, 122

Tannenbaum-Schmidt's Continuum, 14

Target stage (TEACHER model), 62

    contracting, 65–6

    environment, 64–5

    expectations, 67–8

    goals, 68

    pleasantries, 65

    pre-meeting, 62–3

    time management, 67–8

    trust, 66–7

teaching styles, 1–3

team coaching, benefits of, 51–2

team learning, 52–3

team relationships, stages of, 51

team roles, effective, 50

teams types, 49–52

technological advances, impact of, 40

teleology, 96

T-GROW model, 30–1

think-blink technique, 87

360 feedback, 16

time culture, 136–7

time management, 67–8

time orientation, 137

total quality management (TQM), 106–7

transactional analysis (TA), 142

transformational leadership, 108

trust, 66–7

uncertainty avoidance, 133–4

verbal communication, 141–2

visualisation, 95–7

waves of trust, 66

well-being, 47–8

Well-being (Robertson and Cooper), 48

wheel of life, 69–70

WOOP coaching model, 32–3

For Product Safety Concerns and Information please contact our EU
representative GPSR@taylorandfrancis.com
Taylor & Francis Verlag GmbH, Kaufingerstraße 24, 80331 München, Germany

www.ingramcontent.com/pod-product-compliance
Lightning Source LLC
Chambersburg PA
CBHW051745230426
43670CB00012B/2172